PAUL NEWMAN
Superstar

A Critical Biography
by
LIONEL GODFREY

ST. MARTIN'S PRESS
NEW YORK

ROBERT HALE LIMITED
LONDON

ISBN 0 7091 6914 0

Robert Hale Limited
Clerkenwell House
Clerkenwell Green
London, EC1R 0HT

All rights reserved. For information, write:
St. Martin's Press, Inc., 175 Fifth Ave., New York, N.Y. 10010

Library of Congress Catalog Number: 76-66404
First published in the United States of America in 1979
ISBN 0-312-59819-X

Photoset by Ebenezer Baylis & Son Ltd.,
The Trinity Press, Worcester.
Printed and bound in Great Britain by
Weatherby Woolnough, Northants.

Contents

Author's Note

Before this book was written, I informed Paul Newman of my intentions and invited him to co-operate, at least to the extent of supplying detailed comments on his view of acting in general and, more specifically, on the roles he had played. He declined, but took pains to explain that though he did not wish to be unhelpful, he had no desire to participate in the composition of any biography (or, indeed, autobiography).

The reader should therefore not interpret the use of first names in the text that follows as proof of personal intimacy. However, after thinking and writing, about Paul Newman and Joanne Woodward day after day over many months, I eventually found it unnatural to maintain a formal distance in print. By all concerned, especially my subject and his wife, I hope that any degree of familiarity will be seen only as that of respect and admiration.

L.G.

Introduction

'Probably many others feel about Paul Newman as I do', wrote Pauline Kael, the shrewdest, most discriminating and best of American movie-critics. 'I like him so much I always want his pictures to be good, for his sake as well as for my enjoyment.' Such is the drawing-power of a superstar, and Paul Newman is nothing if he is not a superstar. In other words, before the game ever begins, the crowd is rooting for its idol to score again.

But if anyone can be *more* than a superstar, Newman is much more than what meets the eye on the cinema-screen – glamorous and arresting though the image may be. 'I don't know a woman or a girl-child who doesn't ordinarily enjoy looking at Paul Newman', wrote Pauline Kael, but she herself, sometimes mercilessly, is capable of dissecting his performances over many columns of print – simply because they *are* performances, not the standard routines of many other stars who do little more than show their pretty faces. He may be a natural screen-personality, one of those actors whom the camera loves, but he is also a painstaking, intellectual player who works steadily to build up a characterization. 'Paul Newman . . . is terribly good', Tennessee Williams has said. 'He works up to a part slowly, but when he finally gets to it, he's marvellous.' Physically, Newman has a great deal to offer – the much-sighed-over looks, the famous blue eyes, the physique that prompts moviemakers to have him remove his shirt so frequently. But his public respects him as much for his talent as for his handsomeness. 'Women don't try to steal a lock of his hair or tear his clothes off as they do with younger idols,' Barbara Rush, his co-star in *The Young Philadelphians*, once pointed out. 'I think they have too much respect for him.'

And she was right. When, during the shooting of *The Towering Inferno*, Newman strayed outside a police-cordon protecting the moviemakers and strolled in the streets, the people did not mob him but merely applauded politely. Perhaps the power he projects on the screen helped to hold them in check, for he is not only adored by women but also admired by men. 'He makes you listen to him,' said another co-star, Janet Leigh. 'He demands a response.' That screen-presence is an unusual mixture — a combination of toughness and vulnerability, of the traditionally masculine and the unexpectedly feminine. Small wonder that his appeal is virtually universal. Even at the outset of his career, Victor Saville, who directed the biggest flop in which the star ever appeared, discerned that Newman had 'an intensity and strange sense of brooding that come over on the screen with a terrific impact'.

The praise, however, has not been unanimous. In the early years especially, reviewers were eager to dub him a cut-rate, imitation Brando, but though such voices have generally been silenced after two decades, the critic David Thomson, writing comparatively recently, could still deride 'the uneasy mixture of porous cockiness and mumbling naturalism'. Among critics, Newman has paid, too, for his looks, as though so handsome a man could not possibly be a fine actor as well. Again, David Thomson categorizes him as 'essentially an uneasy self-regarding personality, as if handsomeness had left him guilty'. If there is a small grain of truth in the charge, it lies in Newman's hypersensitivity to praise for his good looks. He would much rather be valued for his ability, and though he has yet to win an Academy Award, he has had his way. After *Hud*, *The Hustler* and *Hombre*, few dared ever again to describe him as *just* a filmstar.

He is, as this book will endeavour to show, a man of paradoxes and contradictions. Paul Newman the great sex-symbol is a contented family man, devoted to his wife Joanne Woodward and to his children. In an age when the star addicted to seclusion is fast becoming a cliché, he was the first to erect insurmountable barriers of privacy that evoke memories of a previous era and Greta Garbo. His first marriage failed, but his second has been a model of durability and constancy, weathering all outside attacks from those who have maliciously reported its imminent collapse — no doubt perversely hoping that the wish could make it so. Newman devotes his energies to such mundane, unspectacular interests as ecology, politics and education, but he also spends much of his time motor-racing, in which, at an advanced age for the sport, he has shown genuine talent. In almost every way, he seems impervious to the passing years, and there are those whom it is hard to convince of the fact that he is well into his fifties.

Newman's gift for the drama has turned out to be dazzlingly protean — adaptable to a variety of functions. As actor, he has returned repeatedly to the stage, a medium far less protected for a performer than the cinema, and he has triumphed there at least twice. As a movie-producer, he has taken gallant risks with unusual projects. He has not only acted magnificently on the screen but has also directed with undeniable flair and distinction such films as *Rachel, Rachel* and *The Effect of Gamma Rays on Man-in-the-Moon Marigolds*. Another director, the great John Huston, though he was at the time considering Newman primarily as a star, has said, 'Paul Newman is full of innovation. He has wonderful immediate ideas. Very often supplements mine, or has something better than my notions. Some action, perhaps.'

If, according to one theory, Newman may be among the last of his line, this is the age of the superstar, and he is perhaps the greatest of superstars. Ordinary people have always needed their idols, and good looks have ever proved more fascinating than good works or rare gifts. That Paul Newman has combined all three is a cause for celebration, and, among celebrities, it would be hard to find a better hero.

1

Who is Paul Newman?

In a typically magnanimous assessment, another star, David
Niven, sketches Paul Newman with brevity and clarity: 'He is a
dedicated professional, totally understanding and generous in
his work with others, has a wild sense of humour and somehow
manages to consume enormous quantities of beer without
putting on a single ounce! It is a lasting disgrace that this
splendid actor, for some reason, has not yet been awarded an
Oscar. He has done more good for Hollywood movies and
therefore for the world of films than anyone else I can think of
since the great studios virtually collapsed.'

So speaks one professional of another. Other people, however, almost invariably begin with Newman's appearance.

For many, the first and last impression is of phenomenal
good looks. Well into his thirties and beyond, Paul Newman
had the features of a Greek god, and thus Hollywood, predictably taking its cue from externals, began his screen-reign
in 1954 by casting him as a Greek sculptor in *The Silver
Chalice*, a $4½ million flop that might well have finished the
illustrious career it was just starting. With the passing years,
the flawless profile has weathered, of course, and the lines its
owner has acquired have turned the face over which women
throughout the world have sighed into an appropriately
interesting map of experience. Nevertheless, both Newman
and his admirers are haunted by his breathtaking handsomeness, its least changing ingredients being the eyes and their
challenging blue, the strength of his jaw, his sensitive mouth
and a comparatively short, jutting nose. Despite middle-age,
the profile is still impeccable. Paul Newman, like it or not, is,
if not the world's greatest male sex-symbol, certainly among
the three greatest.

He probably does not like it all that much. The shrug with
which he acknowledges the results of popularity-polls,
pointing out quietly that he is a happily married man, may be
careless but is also partly made up of impatience. His manner

implies that if the world has not yet realized that Paul Newman Sex-Symbol is also a passable actor, then so much the worse for the world, and he has repeatedly scoffed at the fabled blue of his eyes — as though if their colour changed to-morrow, he would be any better or worse a performer. The more thoughtful of his admirers would agree with him. When Warnercolor first captured the hue of his eyes in 1954, it proved then and there, despite the inadequacies of *The Silver Chalice*, that Warner's new star could inspire the required swooning response in women-fans. That sort of naïve reaction had to sustain a Tyrone Power throughout his career. But in the near-quarter-century since Newman began, he has earned — through the painstaking perfection of technique, the dedicated preparation for his roles and the customarily careful selection of films — a more critical appraisal and an evaluation of his qualities that is not couched in the fulsome prose of fan-magazines or based purely (or impurely) on the evidence of box-office receipts.

For Paul Newman is that rare combination — both a super-star and a player of demonstrated versatility. He may be type-cast, but he has no need of typecasting; and even as the record stands, his *range* of roles is interestingly wider than that usually associated with stars. Those who have tried to label him as a typical star point out that his parts have permitted only limited variation; the unifying factors in them have been marked — drive, ambition, rebellion, alcoholism, egoism and martyrdom. But the terms in the list are infuriatingly vague, and their obscurantism suggests a much narrower span than the one within which Newman has really acted.

True, he has seldom sought to disguise rare good looks, so that he has the arguably limiting handsomeness of a star, but it is nonetheless hard to define the 'typical' Paul Newman role. If there is one — and the quest to discover it may be a meaning-less exercise — it is perhaps that of the loner. Hud is 'a bastard' (Martin Ritt's label); John Russell in *Hombre* is a morally pure, uncorrupted man; Rocky Graziano in *Somebody Up There Likes Me* is a blindly aggressive rebel; Ed Hall Jr in *The Rack* is a morally tormented collaborator; Fast Eddie Felson in *The Hustler* is a perfectionist with the drive of a great artist; the author in *The Prize* is a hard-drinking cynic; Hank

Stamper in *Sometimes A Great Notion* is a disciple of self-reliance; Anthony Judson Lawrence in *The Young Philadelphians* is a materialistic opportunist (though not a whole-hearted one); Ari Ben Canaan in *Exodus* is a fervent believer in isolationism ('When the showdown comes, we will always stand alone. . . . We have no friends except ourselves.'); Cool Hand Luke is a symbol of man's indomitability. What these diverse characters have in common is that they expect — and usually get — help from nobody; they are essentially alone with a solitariness that is summed up at its bleakest by Hud Bannon's remark: 'You don't look out for yourself, the only helping hand you'll ever get is when they lower the box.'

Of course, we return to the inescapable fact that Newman, unlike a Paul Muni, has almost always *looked* the same — a unifying factor in itself. Those blue eyes about which he is so defensive are reassuringly evident in picture after picture. But they, and the impeccable Greek profile, are probably less restricting than a charm and vulnerability that Newman either cannot or will not suppress.

It is a theme to which we shall repeatedly return.

There is no denying Newman's sex-appeal, his enormous animal attractiveness, but, charm aside, his appearance is relatively unconventional. He certainly does not look like a gentleman-star in the mould of Ronald Colman. On the other hand, his appeal is not that of Clark Gable, a good-looking artisan. That essentially proletarian allure finds more recent embodiment in Steve McQueen, who, like so many other stars before and since, reveals strikingly the truism that a mass-audience most frequently identifies with physical types who imply commonplace, unremarkable qualities.

In what way, then, is Paul Newman different? Film-makers, it might be pointed out, have been quick to exploit his obvious physical attributes, and the preoccupations of *machismo* are to be seen in many of his roles, even if they lack the same simple-minded dedication to masculine toughness that Gable's films had. As a man, Paul Newman is not renowned for his intellectual pursuits.

But when he emerged in the mid fifties, the star was well named. The persona he projected was stimulatingly innovatory. While nobody doubted his masculinity, it was possible to imagine this star reading a book, listening to Bach, delivering a talk, even shedding tears. John Wayne had never prompted such visions. Indeed, nobody before Newman, not even Brando, had done much to erode the seemingly indestructible stereotype of the two-fisted, hairy-chested male. Newman himself, it must be admitted, had to pay homage to that stereotype — perhaps not too ungrudgingly — and in later years he has returned to it with his portraits of a racing-driver, a lumberjack and an ice-hockey player; but early in his career, he undoubtedly rocked the granite monolith on its pedestal, pioneering for the Hoffmans and the Benjamins to topple it, before it was once more set fair and square by the enormously popular *macho* idols Charles Bronson and Clint Eastwood.

If his star-roles up to 1959 had only occasionally been unusual, Paul Newman was at that period something new in stars. His timing was good. He offered himself to a nation prepared to admire with the sort of adulation normally reserved for moviestars a presidential candidate and later a president who, in the person of John F. Kennedy, presented himself as young, clean-cut, well read and a patron of the arts. (Of course, the reality was somewhat different.) Why should not the same nation readily accept a star who could play engineers, authors, scientists and lawyers as well as outlaws, prize-fighters and con-men? American stereotypes were not being abandoned, but new models were being evolved.

That was all twenty years ago. Since then, Newman's fluctuating career has perhaps become more conventional, especially in the late sixties and the present decade. He rounded off ten years of triumphant critical and popular success by being No. 1 at the US box-office in 1969 and 1970, but he slipped to No. 3 in 1971, and after *Cool Hand Luke* (1967), there had been an almost inevitable decline in the excellence of his roles, if not in his playing of them. Moviegoers were responding to a different type of hero. Dubious European models set the tone for ambiguous acting-styles that blurred instead of defined characters.

Not that Newman did not make adjustments that ensured a resurgence of popularity to new heights. They were heights, however, at which he could do little to delight those who venerated him as an actor, for hugely as *Butch Cassidy And*

The Sundance Kid in 1969 and *The Sting* in 1973 pleased their public, neither picture offered the complexity and riches of such earlier works as *Hud, Hombre and The Hustler*. The superstar had earned the right to relax a little; and perhaps he did.

The judgement has to be tentative, for Newman's interests during the seventies have arguably been either widely dispersed or aimed at other areas than the vertiginous heights of superstardom. A family man, he is happily married, with three children by his first wife and three daughters by Joanne Woodward to take up some of his time and energies. In 1968, he enjoyed the creative experience of directing his wife in *Rachel, Rachel*, a widely acclaimed picture. After the film's success, he formed the Newman-Foreman company and in 1969 made the limp *Winning*, in which he co-starred with Joanne Woodward but did not direct. Part of the idea was to have fun racing cars, a hobby of Newman's along with riding motorbikes. In 1970, when *Sometimes A Great Notion* ran into trouble, he took over the direction, and though the film itself was no great shakes, he removed any possible doubts about his ability to direct, which he demonstrated yet again in 1972 by directing his wife in *The Effect Of Gamma Rays On Man-In-The-Moon Marigolds*. Politics, too, were another active interest, and both he and his wife have been among the Hollywood celebrities involved in the civil rights movement — perhaps with a more personal identification than others who merely took up a modish cause. In 1968, when Eugene McCarthy ran for President, Newman campaigned full-time for him. He has denied, however, that, like Ronald Reagan and George Murphy before him, he has any wish to move over to politics.

On the contrary, he repudiates the notion of the deep political thinker just as he rejects so many other stereotypes into which people would like to fit Paul Newman. He marvels that equal attention is not paid to his sense of fun. Above all, he refuses to comply with or correspond to the image of himself as one of the world's great sex-symbols. In this refusal, he is aided and abetted by Joanne Woodward, who, with her well developed sense of humour, will point out that he is in his fifties and snores.

In that combination of chronological data and domestic detail is more than a hint of the great paradox that is Paul Newman. Now in his middle-fifties, he maintains and enhances his allure, and yet not only does he fail to work at projecting the superstar-image, but he also does a great deal — if involuntarily — to discourage it. Paul Newman the Star belongs to the world, but Paul Newman the Man is an extremely private person, notoriously reluctant to give interviews or to lead the life of a Hollywood celebrity. What details of the man's *modus vivendi* and marriage do emerge tend to conflict with or dispel the screen-aura.

Like Steve McQueen's similar addiction to roaring motors, Newman's fondness for racing cars may have its elements of glamour, but there is also a little-boy allure about it that reminds us that the blue of his eyes is the blue of childhood. (Those eyes, extremely sensitive histrionic instruments, should not be underrated, however: their effect can be jolting and disturbing.) The screen rebel, loner and lover finds a provocative contrast in the contented family-man, gregariously sitting in the kitchen, chatting and occasionally reaching for a beer from an ice-box crammed with cans. He and Joanne explicitly hate the false existence of the movie-colony, the Newmans' base being Westport, Connecticut, and perhaps in retaliation, Hollywood gossip has more than once — notably in the mid seventies — alleged that they were splitting up. Nearly twenty years old, the marriage survives and flourishes.

Scandal has never touched the mature Newman. There is nothing exotic either in his life-style or his antecedents — good middle-class stock, without another actor in sight. He seems to be the least pretentious of men. All the more remarkable, then, that his stature as a star is so great and that his accomplishments as an artist have been much more impressive than his critics will allow.

Actors are paid to be someone they are not, and only the incurably naïve can continue to marvel that Paul Newman is not Hud, that he does not have a roving eye like Andrew Craig in *The Prize* or that he is not an unrelenting hard man like Hank Stamper in *Sometimes A Great Notion* or a little-boy-lost like Billy Bonney in *The Left-Handed Gun*.

Has Newman then no secrets?

Naturally, he must have. But perhaps the greatest of them is an open one. He works at his trade. He is an assiduous observer of people, and he studies hard in his preparation for his roles. Never pretending that acting comes easily to him, he has conquered or at least mastered his diffidence, the quality he once feared would most seriously mar and impair his acting. In his art, he shows a less spectacular courage than the daring he exhibits on the track, but it is just as real. Compared with Brando (and many have made the comparison — usually to Newman's disadvantage), he may look ultra-conservative, but he has taken risks, even if they have been calculated ones, such as playing an out-and-out heel in *Hud*. His tackling the role of Juan Carrasco in *The Outrage* indicated his willingness to attempt the new and the challenging, and there was undeniable bravery in turning his back on Hollywood after it had got him off to a bad start in 1954. Materially, he had a great deal to lose.

Stardom is inimical to virtuoso acting. Even with the collapse of the studio-system, the same sort of thinking persists — mainly because it encapsulates a pragmatic, virtually unchallenged truth: a mass-audience must identify with its idol, and it can best do so via films designed to exploit only the most obvious and familiar facets of his personality and looks. It follows that the star who has aspirations towards versatility is inevitably frustrated, since his range will be restricted by the vehicles in which he appears. Thus on a 'new-style' superstar like Paul Newman, his career largely *after* the break-up of the old Hollywood studios, the same principles impinge that affected the traditional superstar like Clark Gable. Significantly, both men have played racing-motorists — roles that are a sure index of the *macho* star. Presumably because he has not wanted to, Newman has not completely escaped such thinking; but it is to his credit, as we shall see, that he has considerably *widened* the range normally associated with a star of his type and magnitude.

The other pressures of stardom he has coped with even more decisively. Newman's aversion to intrusive publicity and exposure has already been indicated. He has protected himself and those whom he loves. But all the pressures have been doubled, it should be borne in mind, for Joanne Woodward is

an actress of formidable talents and undoubted success. At
different times, the Newmans' careers have been both separate
and joined, bad luck generally dogging their co-starring
appearances, especially in comedy. On the other hand, the
occasions when Paul has directed Joanne have been fruitful for
all concerned.

One showbiz school of thought asserts that there are no co-
stars in a marriage: it is safer for a star to marry a 'civilian' or
non-professional; or if two stars *must* marry, one career should
take precedence over the other. It might be said that the
Newmans have kept the last provision in mind and that if anybody's career has come first, it has definitely been Paul's. But
it is equally obvious that the juxtaposition has not been oversimplified to black and white, either/or. In her own right,
Joanne has had a remarkable professional life, with little
danger of being stifled or eclipsed by her husband. In 1977,
explicitly acknowledging whose ambitions had been allowed
unhindered development, Newman announced that he would
take a year off to give more scope and freedom to 'one of the
best actresses in the business'. For her part, his wife admitted
that much as she loved being Mrs Paul Newman, she also
enjoyed being Joanne Woodward. Thus intelligently, with
give-and-take, mature concessions, one of the cinema's most
celebrated couples have dealt with the combined demands of
their stardom. They have defended their marriage and family
not only against pressures from without but also against the
often subtler ones from within. Each partner has a well
nourished sense of identity, and if Joanne complains that when
the two of them go to parties people have a habit of saying,
'Look, there's Paul Newman. Who's that with him?', her
tongue, it might be judged, is lodged with some firmness in
her cheek.

Alienation and success are two of the great themes of
twentieth-century life and art. The first will be found as a
recurrent motif in the films of Paul Newman. The second can
be seen just as surely in his life and career.

When he returned to Hollywood after the débâcle of *The
Silver Chalice*, he was prepared if not to slay the giant at least
to give it a good fight. Perhaps he was not always successful,

and certainly his struggles have been minimized. But in the next two decades, he was a superstar, the world's most popular actor. He himself has asserted that no one in such a position could avoid being typecast, but if he has been, the inevitable process has taken place within a range that has been surpassed only by an élite that includes Olivier and Brando among the living and Paul Muni and Edward G. Robinson among the dead. Unlike Dorothy Parker's actress who 'ran the gamut of emotion from A to B', Paul Newman is in august company.

2

From Shaker Heights to Hollywood

There is an old, old joke about a city slicker visiting a rural community who asks a hayseed, 'Any great men born hereabouts?' — to be put down by the instant retort: 'Nope. Only babies.'

Paul Newman started life merely as a baby and enjoyed a childhood that was distressingly uncolourful — at least by the standards of studio-publicists. Many legends begin small, and there was nothing in Newman's early years to hint at the great things to come. He was born on 26th January 1925, in Cleveland Heights, Cleveland, Ohio, to Arthur S. Newman and his wife Theresa (*née* Fetzer). Arthur Newman was of German-Jewish stock and was secretary-treasurer of the Newman-Stern Company, which was a successful sporting-goods concern. Like her husband, Theresa Newman was a second-generation American, the product of a Hungarian Catholic family. Later, however, she was converted to Christian Science, and it was in this faith that her son Paul was reared, though its teachings, as Newman has since confessed, made no real impression on him — certainly none that has lasted.

Soon after Paul's birth, the Newmans — including Paul's brother Arthur, who is a year older — moved to Shaker Heights, where Theresa Newman still lives. This was a better district, an upper middle-class milieu, with secluded properties and well tended gardens. Paul Newman was thus to grow up in comfort and muted affluence. Any note of conflict or division in his formative years came, as it so often does, from the parents, whose influence upon him, if it did not actually pull in opposite directions, at least developed two different sides of his character that he was later to combine in some of his most famous roles.

Like father, like son; and Newman as a boy was interested in sports, as, predictably, was his father. Almost as predictably, the artistic instincts of the boy were encouraged if not implanted by his mother, in whom, Newman has since hinted, there were ambitions to act that had never been realized. At any rate, she would attend the Hanna Theatre in Cleveland, where she was enthralled by the productions. Somewhat surprisingly, though, she never took along with her the younger son to whom she liked to describe the plays in detail.

At her prompting, however, Paul joined what has variously been described as 'The Curtain Raisers' or 'Pullers', a children's sub-division of the Cleveland community theatre. When he was twelve, he performed as St George in *St. George And The Dragon*, pouring salt on the dragon's tail. This, it might be supposed, was his first starring-role, but five years earlier, aged seven, he had played a court jester in *The Travails Of Robin Hood* and yodelled a song composed by his uncle, Joe S. Newman, a journalist and poet. Paul had one entrance and one exit, and though this early performance was his first big hit, especially with his family, he recalls finding the experience disturbing and uncomfortable.

In amateur theatricals, the young Newman manifested a facility that had no counterpart in his sporting activities. Although he played football, baseball and basketball, Newman has admitted that he was not a distinguished athlete. One might allow for some minimizing modesty in the assertion, but he has also said that he was an unusually clumsy young man.

With hindsight and the knowledge of his mature professional and personal self-discipline, perhaps the most striking feature of Newman's upbringing was its relative strictness. Given different parents and the same material circumstances, he might easily have been spoiled, but there was no hint of excess or indulgence in the manner in which Theresa and Arthur Newman reared their son. Later, for Hollywood, it might have been expedient and exploitable if Paul had been a juvenile delinquent, if he had worked as a truckdriver, lumberjack and oil-rigger. By showbiz standards, his background might have been square, but it provided him with the stability to withstand the disorientating nonsense of a sphere whose casualty-rate is notoriously high.

Paul was educated at the local elementary schools and Shaker Heights Senior High School, from which he graduated in January 1943. While there, though with no thought of a subsequent career in acting, he stage-managed and appeared in plays, not always getting the parts on which he had set his sights. For example, he failed to secure the role of First Grave-digger in *Hamlet* — an odd choice for a very young man.

That Paul should eventually enter the family business had long been taken for granted by the entire Newman clan, uncles and all. But after graduation, he enlisted in the navy, and while he was waiting to be called for flight-training, he attended Ohio University, in Athens, Ohio, for four months — in his own words, majoring in beer-drinking. Acting was still a casual, undemanding hobby. In the Speech Department's production of *The Milky Way* by Lynn Root and Harry Clark, he played one of the leads — Speed McFarland, the middle-weight champion. (Producers were already spotting an obvious way of capitalizing on his fine physique.)

After he had been selected for the V-12 programme, the navy eventually sent Paul to Yale, but his hopes of being a pilot in the Naval Air Corps were dashed when he was dis-qualified in July 1943, for colour-blindness. He then served for nearly three years, mainly in Guam, Hawaii and Saipan, as an aviation radioman, third class, on torpedo-planes. Even so, he saw no combat.

After discharge in April 1946, he went on the G.I. Bill to Kenyon College in Gambier, Ohio, ninety miles south-west of Cleveland, and studied economics for a couple of years before switching to English and speech.

What happened at Kenyon could well have steered him to-wards the activity that was to become his profession and pre-occupation. Perhaps everyone who goes to college dreams of becoming a college-celebrity, and it seemed that Paul had found one road to that goal when he was picked for the second-string football-team. Unfortunately, though, he scarcely excelled at the sport, and when he and some of his team-mates were involved in a bar-room brawl, the man-datory 'youthful indiscretion' of those years, Paul was thrown off the team. Possibly he had a flair for business, after all, because he ran the first student-laundry, and at the same time, having failed in one bid for campus-fame, he joined the drama-group, eventually appearing in more than ten plays and even trying his hand at direction. In retrospect, he insists that his performances in productions such as *R.U.R.*, *The Alchemist* and *Charley's Aunt* qualified him only as one of history's worst college-actors and that his ideas about his craft were crude and rudimentary — little more than a matter of learning his lines and repeating them automatically.

Thus far, his experiments with acting might have been described as arbitrary flirtations, at first urged on by his mother and later, at college, drifted into virtually by accident. He scarcely had the undeflected motivation towards dramatics of, say, a Tyrone Power, a Douglas Fairbanks or a Peter Fonda — famous sons of famous fathers. But, as Pascal has reminded us, by divers means men come to like ends, and Paul's appetite was now truly whetted. Undergraduate success is not to be taken too seriously, and its uncritical acceptance as a foundation for hopes and ambitions has no doubt disillusioned many. But Paul was no fool. By now, he must have been conscious of his looks, and though he had definite reservations about his acting-talent, he could no longer deny that the gift was there — to be exercised and developed if he had the will to do so. And about his tenacity he has never exhibited false modesty.

He has been lucidly, intelligently frank about his problems in his craft. He realized early that he had no intuitive facility — unlike (and the contrast is of his making) Joanne Woodward. For Paul, acting has meant study, a cerebral process that, given his perfectionism, has demanded painful, exacting work. He still asserts that he does not enjoy acting, that preparation gives him greater pleasure, that each new part has required a diligent inquiry into motivation; and if the vocabulary begins to sound familiar, it must be remembered that he was to become a member of the Actors' Studio in August 1952, before his career was very old.

A corollary to his lack of instinctive talent, Paul discovered, was diffidence, his inability to let go. It might have worried him at first in those tyro-performances at Kenyon and even much later, but, looking back, he has probably perceived that this emotional restraint was a handicap that converted itself, by the incalculable chemistry of the art, into a golden asset. For that diffidence is revealed in his finest performances as a form of shyness, a withdrawal even in the act of offering himself. Such reserve, it might be added, has enormously heightened the appeal to women of those phenomenal good looks.

However, the fine performances were in the future when, in 1948, he did a summer of stock in Plymouth, Massachusetts. There was more to come. In the spring of his senior year, he accepted a room-and-board scholarship for summer stock at Williams Bay, Wisconsin. On 13th June 1949, he graduated, and by four that afternoon, he was entrained for Williams Bay, where he debuted in Norman Krasna's *John Loves Mary* before playing the Gentleman Caller in *The Glass Menagerie* by the dramatist who was to be of great importance in his later stage- and screen-career, Tennessee Williams. Hitherto, Paul's most exacting role had probably been as Hildy Johnson, the ace-reporter, in *The Front Page* at Kenyon. In the fall, he joined the Woodstock Players in Woodstock, Illinois, near Chicago, where he met Jackie Witte at the Brecksville Little Theatre while he was starring in one of sixteen productions in which he appeared that included *Cyrano De Bergerac* and *Dark Of The Moon*. Paul fell in love with the attractive Jackie, and they married in December. In the spring, he was working as a labourer on a farm near Woodstock — so far, not seriously troubled by the twin burdens of responsibility and ambition.

Despite these new vistas of personal happiness and fulfilment, this was hardly the most settled period in his life. When his father fell ill in April, Paul returned to Cleveland to run the family business until Arthur Newman died in May 1950 — the same year in which Scott, the first child of the marriage, was born.

To say that Paul gave up, however temporarily, definite plans and ambitions in order to return home would be sweeping. He *still* had not arrived at the firm conviction that acting was his vocation or at least what he could do best, and the immediate post-college period had been one of agreeable coasting, a spell of carefree enjoyment enhanced and intensified by his commitment to Jackie. However, his work with the Newman-Stern Company, which his mother had persuaded him to take on, was to provide the shove he needed. In a sense, that shove was negative: he was getting away from something he hated ('I just couldn't find any romance in it') rather than running to something he loved. For the family business was to present him with some of the unhappiest months of his life, and he knew from his limited experience that acting, even if greasepaint was not in his blood, had to be better than *that*. Part of the irony of his predicament in running Newman-Stern was that he was successful at it.

Paul had yet to find out, in Thoreau's words, 'how to make a living not merely honest and honourable, but altogether inviting and glorious'; but he firmly rejected what the great solitary had called a life of 'quiet desperation'. Though he realized that there was such a phenomenon as the romance of merchandizing, Paul had no feeling for it. When it was agreed that the Newman store should be sold, thus terminating any obligation he might have been presumed to have towards the family business, he tired of hanging around Cleveland, where he had been manager of a golf-range and done some acting on local radio, and joined the Yale School of Drama at New Haven with the conservative notion of returning to Kenyon and teaching speech. He left Cleveland in September 1951, and by then he was twenty-seven, and it was time, if he had not done so already, to settle down. He had the cautious instincts inherited through his middle-class upbringing, and he knew that he had so far done well at leading the happy-go-lucky life — not exactly irresponsible, but without the harsh struggle or stern commitments that encumbered some people.

But during that year, experience and encouragement combined to change his intentions and transmogrify his life. He moved Jackie and the baby to New Haven, where they lived on the top floor of an old wooden house that was occupied by three families. Money was not the least of Paul's worries, and in order to support his small son and wife, he sold encyclopaedias. At the School of Drama, he specialized in directing, but also appeared in six one-act plays and at least four full-length plays, including an original called *Beethoven*, in which he played the composer's nephew — light-years removed from the essentially modern parts that were to make him famous. Even so, his participation in the production aroused the interest of William Liebling, a New York agent who asked Paul to look him up if he ever came to town.

Perhaps with that invitation left dangling as an inducement, the inexperienced actor decided to chance his arm in New York in the summer of 1952, nine months after he had arrived in New Haven. Nevertheless, he was cautious enough to make mental reservations: he would give himself a year, and if he, made no progress in the acting-profession, he would return to Yale for his degree and to the sideline of selling encyclopaedias through which he had once made $900 in ten days.

He was not to suffer for long, however, the privations and rejection that are commonly the lot of the unknown actor. For sixty dollars a month, the three Newmans rented an apartment on Staten Island — chosen not at random but rather because Jackie's aunt lived in that neighbourhood and would undoubtedly assist the struggling couple who could not yet afford a babysitter. Paul returned to what seemed to be his trade — peddling encyclopaedias in a sweltering New York summer.

His day began at eight, when he would take the ferry to Manhattan and do the rounds of the agents, as well as attending any casting-calls, before he returned to Staten Island to hustle the books. Made out of seersucker, his one decent suit creased and wilted in the heat. But after little more than a month, he secured two walk-ons in live television, and for a while it was that medium that seemed to offer most prospects. The early fifties was the era of live TV, an exciting time of pioneering inventiveness in which the great figures among dramatists included Rod Serling, Tad Mosel and Paddy Chayefsky. There can be little doubt that Paul was exhilarated by the feeling of innovation and expansion, to say nothing of the heady risks of live transmission, and he was to work for Playhouse 90, Philco and US Steel, the shows in which he appeared including *The Web*, *The Mask*, *You Are There* and *Danger*. Two of his later television performances merit special mention, if only because they had reverberations in his later screen-career. In a musical version of *Our Town*, he co-starred with Frank Sinatra and Eva Marie Saint, with the second of whom he was again to co-star in 1960 in *Exodus*, their scenes together being among the most valuable assets of a wildly unequal film. Paul received excellent notices for his work in *The Battler*, which was a television adaptation of Hemingway's story. Starting as a punchy bum of forty, the actor showed by way of flashbacks the earlier stages in the deterioration of the character he was depicting — beginning with his prime in his twenties when he is a cocky newcomer to the fight-game. The role in some ways prefigured Paul's great success soon afterwards playing a pugilist in *Somebody Up There Likes Me* for the big screen. Furthermore, he was to repeat the characterization as a 'cameo' in Martin Ritt's film of 1962, *Hemingway's Adventures Of A Young Man*.

However, in 1952, when he began, he appeared first in *The March Of Time*, in which he played an old man applauding at the inauguration of President McKinley — for the fee of seventy-five dollars. By September, he had a running-part in the *Aldrich Family* television-series, but his first speaking-role was in a play called *Tales Of Tomorrow* — unintentionally funny science-fiction. Paul played an army sergeant and had a modest number of lines. Even so, he was all but overwhelmed by nerves.

That fall, he also auditioned successfully for the Actors' Studio, appearing with a girl in a scene from Tennessee Williams' *Battle Of Angels* in which he played Val Xavier. The circumstances were all but prophetic, for several years later, Joanne Woodward, the second Mrs Paul Newman, was to play opposite Marlon Brando's Xavier in *Orpheus Descending*, the movie-version of *Battle Of Angels*. At this period, Paul has since confessed, his most realistic ambition — Actors' Studio notwithstanding — was to become a teacher of dramatics. He had little faith in his ability, and he later said, 'I was an untuned piano'. However, the choice of image is in itself revealing — suggesting a fine instrument that needed adjustment, exercise and the demands of perceptive mentors. All these the Actors' Studio and imminent experience were to provide.

William Liebling, the New York agent, made good on his semi-promise to the Yale drama-student by getting him an appointment with William Inge, the author of *Picnic*. Having read — poorly, in his own opinion — for Inge, Paul read again a month later for the director Joshua Logan. Immediately, he was hired to understudy the leading actor, Ralph Meeker. Scarcely believing his luck or the $150 a week he was to be paid, Paul moved house to Long Island — a relatively cheap yet quiet two-bedroom apartment in Queens Village. For two reasons, Jackie had elected not to continue as a full-time actress. She wished to avoid the divisive tug of careers that can exert itself upon any marriage of professionals, but in any case she was soon pregnant again.

Her husband himself was about to encounter the first great milestone in his career, for after a few weeks of rehearsal, he was promoted, with a fifty-dollar-a-week raise, from understudy to featured player in *Picnic*, which began to take shape in November 1952. This Theatre Guild production of William Inge's play, directed by Joshua Logan, was to open on 19th February of the following year at the Music Box Theatre.

As breaks went, this one was magnificent without being ideal. The role Paul wanted — and there can be no doubt that it is the best male part in the play — had gone to Ralph Meeker. If there is a hero in the drama, it is Hal Carter, played by Meeker in the original production, who is a catalyst not untouched by the reaction that his presence sets up. As Inge's works so often were, the play is set in Kansas, and its preoccupations are typical of this gifted dramatist. He was always fascinated by the theme of women without men, and in *Picnic* he presented audiences with two widows, an acute case of spinsterhood and two households deprived of a male presence — those of Mrs Potts and her invalid mother (an off-stage character), and of Flo Owens, her two daughters Madge (Janice Rule) and Millie (Kim Stanley) and their boarder, a schoolteacher called Rosemary (Eileen Heckart). The setting, predictably, is a small Kansas town, and into the lives of the women comes Hal Carter, a penniless drifter with grand tales of his past and future. In the stage-directions, Inge is quite explicit about his status: 'In a past era he would have been called a vagabond, but Hal today is usually referred to as a bum.' However, even if he is the archetypal American failure, Hal is also the archetypal uninhibited stud, whether he wants to be or not. His presence seems to blow apart these smalltown lives of quiet frustration and deprivation. Rosemary is neurotically incensed by his animal grace; Millie, the younger daughter, sees him as a symbol of the free, unfettered life for which she yearns; and when he leaves, Madge, the two already having become lovers, follows him.

Life, Inge is saying, is often inconvenient, disappointing and full of pain; but life is devoutly to be wished for. It is as though the lives of his women, before the advent of Hal, had been in cold storage. Existence without a man, the dramatist is pointing out, is no good, and Mrs Potts, speaking of Hal, says: 'Everything he did reminded me there was a man in the house, and it seemed good.'

This central role is so well conceived and written that it might almost be described as actor-proof. When the play was filmed in 1956, it went to William Holden, who was manifestly too old for the part. Nevertheless, his performance was its own justification for the casting, presenting, as Meeker's had done on Broadway, a drifter who was ebullient, gentle, ridiculous, sad and yet with a moving realization of his inadequacies and his diminishing chances for happiness.

Even though it might have been written with Paul Newman in mind, who can say now what he would have made of the role at that stage in his career? As things were, he was hired to play Alan Seymour (Cliff Robertson in the film), an unreconstructed square and a thankless part for any actor. Alan is Madge's boyfriend and an old college-chum of Hal, and he of course loses Madge to the tired drifter. As written, Alan, for all his good intentions and sense of fair play, is without depth and resonance. His desire to help Hal comes a poor second to his realization of his erstwhile friend's lack of drive and persistence. In a sense, he is like a bowling-pin — standing there solely with the idea of being knocked over.

Even so, Paul's performance attracted respectful reviews in a part that might well have been overlooked. Richard Watts Jr praised his 'excellent work', and Robert Coleman in the *New York Daily Mirror* also used the word 'excellent'. To a career in the theatre, it was an auspicious start.

While the play was still in its formative stages, Paul was used as a sort of catalyst by Joshua Logan and William Inge. During try-outs, it was observed that audiences failed to identify with Hal Carter, whose bluster and swagger scarcely marked him out as a conventional hero. Paul had already proved an immensely sympathetic player, especially with women-playgoers, and the idea was conceived of giving to him

a key-speech that would establish Hal's genuineness quite un-
equivocally. The ruse worked, and thereafter *Picnic* 'clicked'
with its audiences. Thus, at the virtual outset of his career,
Paul's handsome and plausible advocacy was recognized and
made use of in the theatre.

Picnic enjoyed a well deserved success, ran for fourteen
months and 477 performances and won the Pulitzer Prize.
Paul understudied Ralph Meeker and actually got to play Hal
Carter for two weeks. He also came into daily contact with a
young actress called Joanne Woodward who was understudy-
ing the roles of Janice Rule and Kim Stanley and whom he had
first met on a visit to John Foreman, then his agent, later his
business-partner. Just as *Picnic* marked a significant change in
Paul Newman's professional career, so his meeting with
Joanne Woodward was to lead to a momentous alteration in
his personal life.

Paul's big break with *Picnic* came opportunely in the sense
that his savings were running low and that Jackie would soon
give birth to a daughter, Susan, who was born in 1953.
Beginning to enjoy the assurance of recognition and expand-
ing vistas, he worked continually at the Actors' Studio, to
which he has consistently been generous in attributing the
credit for whatever he has achieved artistically since he began
studying there with Lee Strasberg and Elia Kazan. His friends
and contemporaries at the studio included Rod Steiger, Kim
Stanley, Geraldine Page, Eli Wallach, Anne Jackson and
James Dean, who was to cast a shadow—even posthum-
ously—on Paul's early career.

This, then, was a fertile and exciting period, but it was also,
because of his growing relationship with Joanne Woodward,
perhaps the first really taxing chapter in his personal life,
haunted by feelings that were difficult to handle and conflicts
that offered no prospect of easy solution. True, he had had
problems before. There had been the drinking and mild
scrapes of college—nothing too reprehensible, but enough to
worry the conscience of a well-bred boy from Shaker Heights.
Then there had been his leaving home after his father's death.
His action was wholly justifiable, but he had naturally worried
that it might have been seen as a departure of indecent haste

or, inasmuch as he rejected the family-business, as a turning of his back on filial responsibility.

Real or imaginary, these disturbing errors were nothing compared with the dilemma in which he was to find himself for the next few years. What began as the camaraderie of the theatre during the run of a successful play was to intensify and become more demanding when Paul and Joanne found themselves in Hollywood. For both of them, it was to be a difficult time.

The five years leading up to their marriage began, however, well enough for Paul, and there was a sense of rapid acceleration to his career, made manifest by Theatre World's nominating him, on the strength of his performance in *Picnic*, as one of the 'Promising Personalities' of 1953. (A co-nominee was Geraldine Page). He now had encouraging material rewards, a sense of his artistic identity and a growing conviction, largely instilled by his regular sessions at the Actors' Studio, that he was painstakingly learning the techniques and secrets of his craft. But there was even better to come — at least in worldly terms. Towards the end of *Picnic*'s run, Warner Brothers offered Paul a five-year contract at $1,000 per week, and he accepted. In the spring of 1954, he left for Hollywood, and Joanne Woodward followed later in the year to take up a similar contract with 20th Century Fox. Appearing as an adolescent in television's *Four Star Playhouse*, she had aroused the interest of Buddy Adler, who was the studio's head of production.

'*Le destin est railleur!*' ('How fate loves a jest!') says Cyrano de Bergerac in Rostand's play; and fate was certainly ensuring that Paul and Joanne were not to remain apart, even though she was later to recall that they 'ran away from each other for six years'.

Before he did much more than dabble his toes in acting, Paul Newman had been twenty-four — arguably a little late for commencing a theatrical career. By the age of twenty-eight, making up for lost time, he was appearing in a hit-play on Broadway. Next, close to the round number of thirty, he was to tackle Hollywood, and though still a young man by the standards of most spheres, even in an age when the cult of youth was getting into high gear, he was perhaps coming to the big screen later than most who became stars in that era.

It is interesting to compare him with those who, rightly or wrongly, have been mentioned in the same breath with him. James Dean was in movies by the time he was twenty and was starring before he was twenty-five. (Indeed, he was still only twenty-four when he died in September 1955, the day after shooting had finished on his last picture, *Giant*.) Marlon Brando came to the cinema in *The Men*, made before he was twenty-five, and confirmed his stardom the following year by recreating his hit stage-performance for the movie of *A Streetcar Named Desire*. His first association with Broadway, though possibly not so auspicious as Paul Newman's, had been at the age of twenty. Warren Beatty was in his early twenties when he was spotted by William Inge and Joshua Logan, the same men who had been behind *Picnic*, and cast in Inge's *A Loss Of Roses* (the play that, as a film, was to star Joanne Woodward), and his movie-debut, a year later, was in *Splendour In The Grass*, also written by Inge. Only Tony Franciosa paralleled Paul at all closely in the matter of first screen-appearance, for he was nearly thirty when he made *A Face In The Crowd*.

There can be no law about such statistics, but it might at least be suggested that Paul Newman was, for that era, mature to be having his first brush with Hollywood. Of course, styles change, and since the sixties, we are now again used to such older men as James Coburn, pushing forty before he achieved authentic stardom, and Lee Marvin, whose experience was much the same. Coburn, let it be said, played supporting roles for five years, and Marvin took more than twice as long to graduate to star-parts. Their histories make what was to happen to Paul look sudden, if not instant.

For a crack at film-stardom, he had been prepared not so much by his work in the theatre as by his appearances before the television-camera. Even though it must be regarded as beyond the scope of this volume to expatiate on the differences between acting for the stage and acting in movies, a note on the clearer distinctions between the two crafts might at this juncture be useful.

In the cinema, preconceptions about theatrical playing have to be abandoned. Not only is the *need* for such technical assets as impeccable diction far from axiomatic; the broader gestures and expressions of the theatre also become positively grotesque before the camera. (Hence the explanation of the mirth often unintentionally provoked by the acting in silent movies, which, to combat the lack of speech, had a plasticity that has long since become unacceptable on the screen.) If cinema-acting does not require a completely different grammar and vocabulary, then it is at least essentially a matter of underplaying, epitomized by the oft quoted: 'Less'. Here is an art whose vocabulary includes such comparatively subtle devices as the lift of an eyebrow, the shrugging of shoulders and the twitching of lips — to say nothing of such 'naïve', spontaneous bits of acting, there merely for the recording by hypersensitive sound- or camera-equipment, as mumbling or scratching. In a theatre, such details never get beyond the fourth row of the stalls. Acting and the great stars have often combined in a strange chemistry: many of the stars lacked training or were never serious students of their craft, but this very absence of conscious technique had a habit of proving a formidable asset in a business in which looking the part and the ability to relax before the camera were discovered to be of greater importance than *acting* the part.

Of all this, Paul Newman had more than an inkling, if still a great deal to learn, when he set out for Hollywood. It should not be forgotten that one of his teachers at the Actors' Studio was Kazan, who besides being a distinguished director of new plays on Broadway, which he had conquered in the mid forties, was at that time coming into his own as a movie-director by following such relatively muted, gauche films as *Pinky* and *Gentleman's Agreement* with the strikingly personal work, stamped with his characteristic emotional impetus, with which he began the fifties — *Panic In The Streets*, *A Streetcar Named Desire* and *Viva, Zapata!*. As well as one mentor with proven flair for handling actors in the cinema, Paul Newman had a second whose hour was yet to come and did so, largely with Paul as his star, after he had graduated from the small to the large screen in the mid fifties.

Martin Ritt began his professional life as an actor on Broadway, but became an actor-director in television until, blacklisted in 1951 during the hysterical reign of Senator Joe

McCarthy, he took on miscellaneous work to support his
family, one of his activities being the teaching of classes at the
Actors' Studio attended by Paul, Joanne Woodward and Rod
Steiger. Later, able to direct again and in a position to make
films, he was to remember and use the talents of Paul and
Joanne.

Lee Strasberg, Kazan and Ritt — these are formidable
names; and since two of the men between them could royally
supplement Paul's not inconsiderable television-experience, he
no doubt took up his Warner contract with more than a
modicum of confidence in his ability. He had, however, less
than a suspicion that his first sojourn in Hollywood was to be a
virtually unmitigated disaster. If he had made it to film-
stardom before he was thirty, it was an achievement in which
his screen-debut was to leave him little pride.

3

Professional Success, Private Problems

When, after he had become a household-name, Paul Newman's first picture, *The Silver Chalice*, was scheduled for a week on television in Los Angeles, he took out a black-bordered advertisement in the Press saying: 'Paul Newman apologises every night this week — Channel 9.' He explained the gesture as a joke, but if it was, it was a curious one. If, on the other hand, the advertisement was serious, he had nothing about which to apologize. In the career of every star, there are bummers — those pictures he did not want to do but was compelled to do; the productions with the parts that nobody could *make* good; the films that looked sound on paper but turned sour in the making; the movies with roles to which the star was ill suited; the ones in which, rightly or wrongly, he was just going through the motions to work out a contract.

Joke or not, the advertisement was a revealing episode in the life of a star who has always exercised a thoughtful, critical approach ('cerebral' is his own word) to his craft. Multi-million dollar flop *The Silver Chalice* might have been, but the histories of stars just as illustrious as Paul Newman had begun equally badly. In the event, his 'joke' backfired, and the film drew one of the highest ratings in the annals of Los Angeles television. It is an appallingly inept picture, however, in which Paul is understandably subdued, if not sullen, but by the time it thudded on to the small screen, the star could have afforded to laugh at it. If he was not doing so, then that funereal advertisement says something for the sensitivity of the actor who inserted it.

Nearer the time, he was probably overwhelmed by the sense of the film's permanence. A motion picture, like a book, lacks the sometimes advantageous ephemerality of — say — the theatre. As Paul surely knew, a theatrical disaster is soon forgotten, even by those who may have cause to gloat over it. The memory of bad television, too, fades almost as rapidly as the image on the screen. But impoverished, inept cinema pops up again and again. Its durability is haunting. It may be dead aesthetically, but it will not lie down.

Given the circumstances of a new career and a novitiate's enthusiasm, Paul might have been forgiven for approaching his first picture in a spirit of optimism or at least trust. But its genesis augured poorly. Successful pictures have been made from bestsellers much less promising than Thomas B. Costain's novel, but the screenplay by Lesser Samuels must have revealed the weaknesses shown so blatantly by the finished film. It was produced and directed by Victor Saville, a British expatriate who had shown some flair in the English films he made in the thirties but whose talent, unlike that of his compatriot Alfred Hitchcock, did not thrive when it was transplanted to the soil of Hollywood. As a producer, he was associated with pictures whose excellence clearly derived from their directors – Sam Wood (*Goodbye, Mr Chips*), Frank Borzage (*The Mortal Storm*) and George Cukor (*A Woman's Face* and *Keeper Of The Flame*). The films he himself directed are inferior by comparison, and just before *The Silver Chalice*, he had produced and directed *The Long Wait*, derived from Mickey Spillane, a work notable only for its crudity and sadism.

Even Warner's $1,000 a week could not compensate an actor of Paul Newman's sensitivity for the fiasco of *The Silver Chalice*, upon which only the strange sets conferred any sort of distinction. In his own words, after seeing the completed film for the first time, he was 'horrified, traumatized'. In it, he plays Basil, a Greek silversmith who, in the midst of a labyrinthine, confused and confusing plot, must choose between his Christian love (Pier Angeli) and his pagan inamorata (Virginia Mayo, incredibly made-up). The picture, dreary and old-fashioned Hollywood *religioso* about the early Christians, eked out with the usual fights, is not even unintentionally funny, and Paul's acting suggests that he found nothing remotely amusing in the proceedings.

No wonder. His career had started and finished, he thought, in one and the same picture.

At 142 minutes, it was too long and cruelly wasted the talents of such splendid players as Alexander Scourby, Joseph Wiseman, Albert Dekker, E. G. Marshall and Jacques

Aubuchon. Jack Palance fared better than most others, playing a pagan magician who, convinced that he is a god, attempts to fly. Palance brings immense relish to a grotesque role that supplies involuntary comic relief.

This farrago was dull and gloomy rather than actively offensive. It may be the poet's secret to touch pitch without becoming defiled by it, but Paul had nothing of which to be particularly ashamed. In terms of physiognomy, he looked ideally cast, even if he wore his robes somewhat uneasily. Not surprising in a newcomer, there were occasional gaucheries, but when his limp part allowed him to show feeling, there were sparks of the characteristic Newman fire and intensity. He may or may not be a poet, but he emerged from *The Silver Chalice* unsullied, perhaps even, to the perceptive, with a little credit.

The trauma of the event lay in the gap between his expectations and the drab reality; in the fact that this was a stultifying, demoralizing beginning; in the descent from being involved, however humbly, in a piece of theatrical history such as *Picnic* to participating in a thick chunk of cinematic trash. The writer Charles Hamblett has reported that he saw Warners' new discovery looking so miserable on the set of *The Silver Chalice* that he did not dare to approach him for an interview. Long before the picture opened, Paul had accepted the disheartening truth.

Warners premièred it on 25th December 1954, and the critics slaughtered it. The year which had begun so bravely and had seen the birth of the Newmans' second daughter, Stephanie, ended with a numbing thud.

But Paul himself was not numbed or paralysed. Once he had seen the film, he made up his mind and wired his agent: 'Get me back on Broadway.' In Hollywood, failure is a disease, and all are guilty by contagion. Paul was smart enough to remember the saying that a star was only as good as his last picture, and he retreated to the New York theatre — a move which, though he had arguably little to lose, took a certain strength.

There are two versions, however, of the exact circumstances attendant on his departure. One has it that his contract gave him the right to do two plays on Broadway. The other suggests that Warners accepted his defection but exacted their own price. What is certain is that the studio tied him to a new seven-year contract, two films a year with an option on a third. Nevertheless, Paul was by this time alert to the dangers. He had learned his lesson via what he called 'the worst motion-picture filmed during the fifties'. There would be no more costume-films; he would never again allow his looks to be exploited rather than his ability as an actor. (He would scarcely have been human, though, if he had set his heart against the exploitation of *both*.)

For *The Silver Chalice* predictably to garner its bitter harvest of bad notices was one thing. But criticisms of his own performance were another — and, in Paul's opinion, often quite unfair. He did not have in mind the pointing out of flaws in acting that he himself called 'very, very bad'. He was, however, upset and irritated by the earliest of many comparisons with Marlon Brando (usually to Paul's disadvantage) that were to dog him for a number of years. Among the reviews that drew attention to the imagined similarities were those by A. H. Weiler of the *New York Times* and John McCarten of the *New Yorker*. Both in acting-style and physical appearance, the resemblances between the two stars were superficial and minimal, mainly a matter of height and build, but 1954 was the year of the two archetypal Brando pictures, *The Wild One* and *On The Waterfront*, and furthermore Warners had launched Paul as a 'second Brando', a ready-made label that gave the critics their cue and did the new star little good in establishing his own identity. Not surprisingly, his relationship with his studio was to be as strained as theirs had been, years before, for Errol Flynn and Bette Davis.

Paul Newman once said, 'All my life I have been extremely lucky — being in the right place at the right time — it's happened so often I can't begin to tell you the whole of it.' In all such careers, good fortune has an important, not to say incalculable, share, and it did not fail him at this point. Hardly had the press torn *The Silver Chalice* apart when on 18th February 1955, he opened in Joseph Hayes' *The Desperate Hours* on Broadway. Once more, he had hitched himself to a theatrical success. The play ran for six months, he had the best role, and he received both adulation (largely among teenage-girls) and rave-notices.

He was not, however, portraying an admirable character, nor did he like the part overmuch. He played Glenn Griffin, the psychopathic leader of a trio of escaped convicts who terrorize the family in whose home they have taken refuge. In casting Paul, the director, Robert Montgomery, was astute, because his youthful appearance and bearing contrasted all the more chillingly with his hardened criminality. (Later, when William Wyler was planning the movie-version, which was released in 1955, he intended to repeat the dramatic coup by casting Griffin in similar vein, but Humphrey Bogart was eager to play yet another mean killer, with the result that Wyler's film, though effective in its own way, was much more conventional.) If the play was little more than unsubtle melodrama, the critics loved Paul's performance in it, and the role was certainly showy enough to be a rising actor's dream. It was the sort of chance that Paul, on the rebound from Hollywood failure, could not and did not let slip.

He also kept looking for work in television. In September, he shed quite a few years to play a high-school student in NBC's musical version of *Our Town*, acting opposite Eva Marie Saint for the first time. The production's narrator was Frank Sinatra. A bigger and better opportunity came his way soon afterwards as a result of James Dean's premature death on 30th September at the wheel of his Porsche Spyder. Dean had been scheduled to play the lead in a television adaptation of Hemingway's *The Battler* that Arthur Penn, later to make *The Left-Handed Gun* with Paul, was to direct for NBC. Having previously been cast as Nick Adams, Hemingway's youthful and autobiographical observer-narrator, Paul was persuaded to take over the role of the eponymous pugilist, and when the show was transmitted live in October, it set up a reaction that was to have a profound effect upon Paul's career.

Watching *The Battler* that night, surely not by chance, were the director Robert Wise and producer Charles Schnee, who had been planning to film *Somebody Up There Likes Me*, the life-story of Rocky Graziano, with James Dean as its star. As they studied Paul's performance on the small screen, they knew that, if he was available, they had their replacement for the newly deceased Dean.

Thus, at this stage in his career, Paul was haunted by two other actors — Marlon Brando and James Dean. While the similarity with Brando was slight, the facile comparisons were predictable, however much Paul detested the 'second Brando' tag. But he was now inheriting parts originally intended for Dean, with whom he had even less in common. Whatever he thought about stepping into a dead man's shoes, Warners were waiting for him to fulfil his contract, and since they themselves had nothing lined up for their new and somewhat incalculable star, they were quite ready to loan him for *Somebody Up There Likes Me* to MGM, who owned the property. Thus, in October, alert and wary, alive to the possibilities of both enormous success and yet another defeat, Paul Newman returned to Hollywood.

Shooting would have begun early in the new year, but near the end of 1955, Glenn Ford pulled out of MGM's *The Rack*, into which Paul was rushed as a replacement. As a film, *The Rack*, with its static camera set-ups and purely functional photography, succeeds only as a good actors' piece and stimulating, if flawed, polemical drama. Nevertheless, even though it does not offer a flashy star-role, it would have made a context for Paul's début vastly superior to *The Silver Chalice*. Written by Stewart Stern and based on a teleplay by Rod Sterling, *The Rack* is literate and sensitive and directed carefully, if not with inspiration, by Arnold Laven. Its principal scenes take place during the court-martial of Captain Ed Hall Jr (Paul), who is indicted for collaborating with the enemy during the Korean War. His defence counsel, Lieutenant Colonel Wasnick (Edmond O'Brien), reveals Captain Hall as one of the first casualties of insidious psychological torture. Without exceptional physical abuse, this military hero, winner of the Silver Star and cluster, son of an army colonel, has been broken by six months of isolation and the subtlest mental torment. Wasnick believes that he has demonstrated convincingly to the court that Captain Hall had reached what he terms his 'horizon of endurable anguish', but in cross-examination, Major Sam Moulton (Wendell Corey) gets Hall to admit that he had not really been driven to his breaking-point but had given up out of fear of reaching it. In a final statement to the court, the accused confesses that he has forfeited his 'moment of magnificence', encountering instead 'a moment of regret that will stay with him for the rest of his life'. The film thus ends, with its echoes of Joseph Conrad, at the point at which the story of *Lord Jim* begins.

Up to this stage, *The Rack* has been a thoughtful, decent picture, with many delicate touches. But having shown persuasively the irresistible pressure of what Wasnick calls 'the new duress', having demonstrated the subtlety with which the Communist torturers have played upon the effects of Ed Hall's loveless upbringing, the film can only disappoint and offend in the ludicrous cop-out of its conclusion — a matter of juggling with semantics. Furthermore, the moviemakers seem unaware that they are depicting a man who is unconsciously using a judicial process to punish himself — a feat he has already accomplished well enough in his own conscience-stricken mind.

Fortunately, the damage is done long after Paul has had chance to create a moving, unusual characterization. Although the role is not the conventional star-part, Paul's performance in it goes far to establish that he is an actor of rare gifts, not afraid to reveal vulnerability and an almost female sensibility.

His restraint and control are so admirable that his emotional outbursts and his breakdowns under questioning, when they come, have a seldom encountered, engaging force. Here is a new contemporary hero — civilized, well-mannered, cultured in speech, articulate and without the boring toughness of so many American males (at least in the cinema). After he has been reunited with a father who would rather salute him than kiss him, he asks his sister-in-law (Anne Francis), 'Are you indestructible, Aggie?' and in the one question conveys to the audience that he and the war-widow are united by the touching affinity of those who have been damaged and know their frailty. 'Why didn't you die?' his father (Walter Pidgeon) demands angrily when he knows of the charges being levelled against his son. 'Why didn't you die like your brother did? It would have been much better that way.' Paul's anguish is beautifully judged as he replies, 'I would have liked it better, too. A nice, clean, acceptable death, with dignity.'

Taking his opportunity from the script, in whose opening

scenes he is an enigma to the audience, he builds up his part steadily and quietly. His manners and self-effacement are protective, but he reveals his disturbed personality in his fear of having other people light his cigarettes — an aversion stemming from the fact, disclosed later, that the most sadistic of his interrogators had performed this service. Without emphasizing the mannerism, Paul is constantly mumbling behind his hand. An army psychiatrist asks him, 'Does it make you feel better to have your hand in front of your mouth that way? . . . Then you're trying to hold something in and your hand helps to do that?' Later, we learn that Ed Hall would bite his hand to keep from answering when his captors asked how he liked solitary confinement.

Before the trial, while he is still recovering from his Korean ordeal in hospital, Ed has a sign stigmatizing him as a traitor slipped over his head while he is watching a movie, and this is the first moment at which Paul's performance is more than muted and self-contained. He attempts to pursue his fleeing accuser (Lee Marvin), and then the agonized tones that a succession of distraught roles are to make impressively familiar are heard for the first time as Ed Hall's cries ring down the hospital-corridor: 'What did you expect me to do? What could I do?'

The screenplay lacks sufficient depth for the character to be complex, but Paul makes the most of the complications in the hero's background, carefully not stressing his lines and thereby courting self-pity, as he explains to Aggie the difference between his own gentler nature and that of his well-meaning but limited and inflexible father: 'My mother wasn't in the army, so I'm a half-breed . . . half my father's disappointment and half my mother's hope.'

Critics were impressed by Paul's handling of an extremely difficult scene in which Colonel Hall, after his son has virtually confessed in court, seeks him out, attempts a reconciliation and tries, after a lifetime of withholding such gestures of affection, to kiss the younger man. Certainly, Paul's acting is excellent as he at first sits stiffly, avoiding looking at his father, and then gradually yields to the man's embrace. But the actor's finest moment is probably in the scene with Aggie that has a two-tier emotional force — drunken musing punctuated by hiccoughs on the surface and a substratum of horror and remorse that finally emerge in a desperate cry as he broods upon the torture-scars, revealed in court that day, of a fellow-officer who did not submit. Before he sobs to Aggie, 'Oh, God! Did you see?', he tenderly, almost unconsciously, comments on the loveliness that, despite her husband's death, blossoms in her: 'Once, I saw an old abandoned apple-farm. . . . But the apples, they didn't know it was abandoned, and they came out anyway, right on schedule. The trees were full, and there was just nobody there to pick 'em. And I thought, My gosh! What a waste!' There, in the midst of this contrapuntal love-scene with the widow of Ed's younger brother, is the apogee of Paul's striking performance — all the more remarkable for occurring amid a feast of fine playing from the other principals.

Naturally, at least one critic talked about 'monotonous sub-Brando' in his acting, and others, using the same insensitive label, derided his mumbling and inaudibility without, apparently, realizing that such incoherence and hesitation were admirable details in the portrait of a man in shock, one who unconsciously sought to muffle his own words. Where Paul's performance might legitimately have been faulted, however, was in his appearance. For a character who had been and still was under terrible strain, the actor looked too well nourished. In the years since *The Rack*, despite David Niven's claim that he can drink copious amounts of beer with impunity, Paul Newman has habitually shed weight for his roles.

The picture contained at least three important pre-echoes of the star's later career. Its screenwriter, Stewart Stern, was also to write *Rachel, Rachel* (1968), Paul's first feature-movie as director. In Ed Hall's crack-up, there are parallels with the crack-up of the eponymous hero in *Cool Hand Luke* (1967), though Luke is broken by a combination of solitary confine-ment *and* physical brutality. And in Ed Hall's background there are suggestions of the antihero in *Hud* (1963), who at one point, charged with being unloved and unlovable, sneers, 'My momma loved me, but she died.' (Ed Hall's mother has been dead years before the action of *The Rack* begins.)

Having premièred *The Rack* in several large cities, MGM appeared to get cold feet and later sat on the picture for a while, believing that it would do better business on national release if *Somebody Up There Likes Me* was shown first.

In that notion, the studio was shrewd, and Paul, leaping at the chance to play Rocky Graziano, had been shrewder. *Somebody Up There Likes Me* was not to be a run-of-the-mill, flat biopic but a finely crafted picture directed by a master, Robert Wise, and written with great insight and humour by Ernest Lehman, whose screenplay derived from the auto- biography upon which Graziano had collaborated with Rowland Barber. Here was the true star-vehicle for which, even though the film had been designed for another actor, Paul's career had been waiting. Yet there was nothing meretri- cious or turgid about *Somebody Up There Likes Me*. As a fifties genre-movie of youth, delinquency and rebellion, it fitted profitably into the canon but nonetheless had its own distinction. While social protest was scarcely its aim, it showed somewhat chillingly that the choice facing the young Rocky Graziano (Paul) was between prizefighting and crime. Its sequences in the ring were excitingly staged (one of the real Rocky's former opponents, ex-middleweight-champion Tony Zale, took part with Paul in the climactic fight), and the central character offered the sort of personality — simple and extrovert — with which a star's fans could readily identify. Paul was relatively young, extremely handsome (though, since the film was in black and white, the later fabled blue of his eyes could not be seen), passionate in his own justification and defence, and apparently handy with his fists. To use a vogue- term, this was a *macho* role, even if it also possessed a tender- ness and sensitivity that were less obvious. Paul, who had looked distinctly flabby in *The Rack*, revealed a fine physique, and since *Somebody Up There Likes Me*, he has never avoided for long the ritual baring of the chest that is obligatory for the super-virile star — as which, paradoxically and interestingly enough, he both does and does not qualify. (Some of these beefcake-episodes are more entertaining than others. In an amusingly transparent sequence, *The Young Philadelphians* has its cake and eats it. Paul plays an earnest, hard-working student of law, but during his college-vacation he gets away from his books and works on a construction-site — divested of his shirt, of course. When another worker offers Barbara Rush an insult, Paul rapidly decks him in good old American style, thereby reassuring the mass-audience early in the picture that beneath all that studiousness and good manners is a two-fisted he-man.)

Like all gifted writers for the medium, Ernest Lehman creates screenplays that, although they may be witty, penetrating and highly literate, are blueprints for directors and actors, not overburdening them with words; and *Somebody Up There Likes Me* is notable for its tautness and economy. The book from which he derives his material may be loose and episodic, but Lehman extracts its most pointed events, presenting them incisively and with a strong feeling for continuity, so that the salient features of Graziano's life emerge with real clarity and dramatic significance — Rocky's slum childhood, surrounded with poverty and crime; his drunken father and long-suffering mother; his helpless delinquency and violence; his incorrigibly rebellious nature ('We'll see whose spirit gets broke,' he declares.); his slow, painful realization that the same violence that gets him into so much trouble can, if used in a socially approved form, earn him wealth and respect — 'the legit' for which he craves.

This last point is summed up and spelled out in a clever speech that Lehman puts into the mouth of an army physical-training instructor: 'You've got something inside of you that a lot of fighters don't have — never will have, no matter how much I teach them. Hate. I don't know why it's there. I only know that if anybody hits you, he better start ducking fast, because that hate pours into that right hand of yours and makes it like a charge of dynamite. A great big waste of a lot of hate. Your whole life you've let it get you into trouble. Why don't you start letting it do some good for you? . . . Be a fighter, Rocky — a professional fighter. . . . Make that hate of yours work for you. Inside the ring, it will make a living for you. Instead of outside the ring, it will just go on lousing up your life for ever. Who knows? It may work so many miracles, you might even lose that hate some day. Is that bad? Maybe you'd just rather go on spitting in your own face for the rest of your life?'

The choice is simple. (Too simple, perhaps. In the cause of effective drama, truth may become a casualty; and there are,

after all, those who grow up in slums to become neither prize-
fighters nor hoodlums, but decent, law-abiding citizens.)
Those of Rocky's buddies who do not or cannot make the
choice end up dead, crippled or rotting in jail. As Romolo (Sal
Mineo), the picture's most pathetic and disturbing character,
says, 'We ain't got a chance, guys like us, do we?'

Thus sharply does Lehman delineate Graziano's character
and milieu; and in the film's later stages, he pinpoints the
irony inherent in the contrast between criminal violence and
legitimate pugilism. When Rocky complains that an opponent
is clobbering him, his manager (a rich portrayal by the great
Everett Sloane) orders, 'Hit him back! It's legal!'

With a sure narrative grasp and impressive economy,
Somebody Up There Likes Me demonstrates Graziano's uneasy
relationship with his parents and charts the juvenile delin-
quencies through which he shows every sign of graduating to
more serious crime. Fighting every inch of the way, he goes
from protectory to reform school to jail until he is finally
drafted into the army, in which he inevitably ends up behind
bars yet again. But at last he has been imprisoned once too
often, realizes why he is there ('for being a dope'), understands
that he can never lick authority with his fists, and plans, not
for the first time, to reform. Leaving the army with a dis-
honourable discharge, he constructively filters his aggression
into prizefighting, aided and encouraged first by his manager
Irving Cohen and then by Norma, the nice Jewish girl later to
become his wife. Though she is at first appalled by the fight-
game, she comes to see that it represents Graziano's salvation,
and the story reaches its climax when he wins the championship. One day, Rocky warns Norma, as they ride in triumph
through New York, he will lose his title and all the acclaim
that goes with it. But that doesn't matter: he has been lucky,
somebody up there likes him. Squeezing his hand, Norma
(gently personified by Pier Angeli) adds, 'Somebody down
here, too'.

Blueprint and character presented a marvellous chance for
any aspirant star, which Paul Newman still was, and he took
that chance in typical fashion. He studied hard to imitate the
real Graziano's speech and physical mannerisms, but his
striking performance implies much more than just a willing-

ness to learn such purely technical matters as a boxer's shuffle and a New York-Italian accent. In Paul's acting, with shoulders hunched partly out of perpetual embarrassment, partly with the instinctive stance of a natural fighter, there is something of the make-up of many young men, particularly in that beautifully observed moment when Rocky, to whom emotions are the least stable of currencies, declares to his girl-friend Norma, 'It's for the birds — I mean, this whole love-business.' His wooing of her, at once comic and touching in its clumsiness, is one of the memorable sequences of an unusual picture. But Paul shows that he can convey a powerful con-viction, too, as Rocky, with what is perhaps his most articulate speech, defends prizefighting to her: 'Maybe it *is* all meanness and blood and ignorance. . . . But where else could a guy like me be something?'

Robert Wise is one of the best cutters in the business, and on *Somebody Up There Likes Me*, he utilized the gifted services of cameraman Joseph Ruttenberg. If *The Rack* had lacked visual distinction, the later film, from its earliest scenes, was stamped with it. A brief prologue acquaints us with Rocky as a small boy — underprivileged, bullied by his father, exhorted to be tough. Apprehended in theft by two cops, he squirms from the grasp of one of them and runs off into the night. One cop makes as if to follow, but the other says disgustedly, 'Save your shoe-leather. There goes another little greaseball on his way. Ten years from now — the death-house at Sing Sing.' Imme-diately, Wise segues to a shot of Rocky, now much older in the person of Paul Newman, still running through the night — 'on the lam' and with every indication of fulfilling the dire prophesy. Wise's neat and taut juxtaposition is quintessentially cinema, almost unthinkable in any other medium.

In a small role in the picture, it might be added, was a then unknown actor later to achieve some fame and to join Paul in an ambitious business-venture — Steve McQueen.

Somebody Up There Likes Me opened in the summer of 1956, and the reviews were ecstatic. At last, Paul was unques-tionably a star. Of course, the Brando-comparisons continued, but this time there was an irony to the parallels drawn between Paul's performance and that of Brando in *On The Waterfront*. There *were* authentic similarities of gait, gesture and speech. With his customary thoroughness, Paul had spent a week with Graziano, studying the fighter's physical mannerisms. What the actor had overlooked or perhaps did not know is best explained in the words of Graziano himself as they appear in the pages of *Somebody Up There Likes Me*:

'This kid took to hanging around me in Stillman's gymnasium, training along beside of me, shooting the breeze. He looked like he might have been a fair fighter once, but he was in bad condition for the ring now and his punch looked slow. I felt sorry for the kid. He rode around town on a second-hand motorcycle, wearing patched up blue jeans. Whenever we went downstairs for a cup of coffee or anything, I always paid for it.

'One day, after he's been hanging around maybe a month, he says come take a walk down Eighth Avenue with him. He takes me into Forty-Sixth Street and points up at the marquee up over a legitimate theatre.

' "Rocky," he says, "that's me. That's where I work. I want you and your wife to come see me."

'Up on the sign it said "Marlon Brando" and the name of the play was *Streetcar Named Desire*.

'When he give me the tickets, he says, "Thanks for everything, Rocky. Thanks." What he's thanking me for, I don't know, unless it's all them cups of coffee . . .

'A few months later I found out why Marlon Brando said thanks to me. I am watching the television, and they introduce this show about fighting and his name is on the screen, and then he comes on and it's me! The son of a bitch is talking like me and walking like me and punching like me! How you like that! I got conned into learning this bum his part by a motorcycle and a pair of blue jeans.'

When one reads that portion of the autobiography, it becomes quite obvious that Brando drew on Rocky Graziano's personality for more than one portrayal, and Paul Newman, having studied the same source, was inevitably thought to be imitating Brando. (Paul himself said that he did not try to *imitate* Graziano — merely to explore a common ground between the fighter and himself so that he could play *a* Graziano.)

Nevertheless, *Somebody Up There Likes Me* was a big enough hit to confer star-status on Paul. For a climax, the film had a thrillingly, not to say electrifyingly, staged fight, for which the actor and Tony Zale had trained hard to attain maximum authenticity, and Paul's role had the physicality that is often so important in attracting masses of fans. Audiences responded instinctively to the picture's graphically demonstrated message that rehabilitation, not punishment, was the lesson of modern penology; even more intuitively, they loved the story of a loser who became a winner; and they identified at once with the star in a performance that modulated convincingly from almost bucolic humour to the moving desperation of Rocky's cry to his mother: 'I tried to turn the leaf, but I can't make it.' For all their tags of 'Brando look-alike', 'Brando-style', 'Brandoesque' and 'tradition of Marlon Brando' (those and other lazy labels appeared in the original reviews), the notices in the press at last admitted that Paul Newman would henceforth have to be considered in his own right.

In the offing was an inevitable return to Warners, but while he waited for a suitable part, Paul kept busy. He had been commuting between the West Coast (filming) and the East (home, Jackie and the children). He filled in the gap in his movie-career with extensive activity in television, appearing in such dramas as *The Rag Jungle*; as a baseball-player in US Steel Hour's Theatre Guild production of *Bang The Drum Slowly* (later filmed for television with James Caan); and again for US Steel in *The Five Fathers Of Pepi*, in which, as one of a quintet of Italian merchants, he had the chance to recapitulate the Italianate acting he had already displayed in *Somebody Up There Likes Me*.

When *The Rack* at last reopened in December, it did so in the shadow of *Somebody Up There* and came and went without leaving much of an impression. As it was a muted and disturbing picture and Paul's performance was remarkable for such uncommercial qualities as dignity, restraint and repression, the comparative lack of response was hardly surprising.

Amidst all this excitement and the burgeoning of his career, there was the stress between his marriage and his attachment

to Joanne Woodward that put him through one of the most
turbulent periods of his personal life, and in 1956 it led him
for the only time into scandal — though on a very minor scale.
On 7th July he was picked up by the police in Mineola, Long
Island, and charged with leaving the scene of an accident and
going through a red light. He had managed to damage
shrubbery and a fire-hydrant, and reports stated that he had
shown aggression, so that the police took him to the station in
handcuffs.

Reputedly, too, he said to one of the patrolmen, 'I'm acting
for Rocky Graziano. What do you want?' By ironic
coincidence, the patrolman's name was Rocco Caggiano
(Graziano's real name was Rocco Barbella), and he replied,
'I'm Rocky, too, and you're under arrest.'

It was an incident to laugh over in later years, an anecdote
to relate to friends or children, a picaresque episode that
might be pasted up in a scrapbook to set off by contrast the
glorious achievements of a great career. But for all its
humorous overtones, the event serves as an index of the private
hell of Paul Newman at that time.

4

Joanne

In the end, it was Jackie who made the decision to divorce, to end with decent finality a marriage at which they had both worked hard — perhaps incredulous at the possibility that they might fail. But circumstances were not easy for anybody. There were Jackie's feelings to consider, the effect on the children to worry about, and for Paul and Joanne Woodward, there was the concern that their love might have the chance to grow without remorse or calumny. All this distress might have been par for the course of marital break-up, yet Paul was no ordinary man but rather a star who loved privacy and had reason to mistrust a Press that had often been hostile, if not malicious. There were always gossip-columnists lurking to make the most and the worst of a bad thing.

In the event, no breath of scandal or sensationalism ever touched any of the parties, and later the shared life of Paul and Joanne was to serve as a model of dignity and wholesomeness.

Even so, events in the mid fifties were leaving their mark on Paul, who was to say of the dissolution of his first marriage, 'I felt guilty as hell about it, and I will carry that guilt for the rest of my life.' Small wonder that he had given so moving a performance as the conscience-stricken Ed Hall Jr in *The Rack*.

For Joanne, it could not have been an easy time, either.

Her attitude could not have been unaffected by the fact that she herself came from a so-called broken home, and what she had observed of the sufferings of her own parents certainly made her unusually cautious in considering matrimony. She was the daughter of Wade Woodward, an affluent publishing executive who had become a vice-president of Charles Scribner's Sons after the Woodwards had divorced. When the marriage foundered, Joanne was brought up by her mother, Elinor Trimmer Woodward, who had been a southern belle in her youth.

Joanne Cignilliat Woodward was born on 27th February

1930, in Thomasville, Georgia, but at the age of fifteen, she moved to Greenville, Carolina, where she worked briefly as a secretary. She was a very bright girl, who developed an outspokenness that was later to make enemies during her early years in Hollywood. After marriage, she retained her sturdy independence of mind, and differences of opinion between her and Paul have often led to large but healthy arguments. She was educated at Louisiana State University, and after two years there, she returned to Greenville and took part in little-theatre productions that included *The Glass Menagerie*. She was a protégée of Robert Machare, a high school drama teacher and little-theatre director. From her childhood, she had been hooked on acting, and her parents wisely did not discourage her. From Greenville, she went to New York, where she did some work for the Neighborhood Playhouse, joined the Actors' Studio and acted extensively in television. In the mid fifties, she was briefly on Broadway with Paul in Leslie Stevens's *The Lovers*.

In 1954, when Buddy Adler earmarked her for a future with 20th Century-Fox, her star, as well as Paul's, was in the ascendant, but complicated circumstances — not excluding marriage, motherhood and the thoughtful weighing of two careers that might have conflicted — ensured that her progress did not exactly keep pace with his. Her career was of course to be punctuated, if not interrupted, by the birth of three daughters — Elinor, born in 1959; Melissa, born in 1961; and Claire, born in 1965. For a variety of reasons, stardom is more hazardous for women than for men. (One of those reasons, recent history has demonstrated, lies in the great imponderable of public taste, and it is particularly ironic that recent years — the apparent peak of female emancipation — have provided so few good roles for women in the cinema.) Luck, too, plays its enormous part, and if Paul was singularly unfortunate in his first film, his future wife was to begin her career even less auspiciously with four indifferent pictures in a row, only two of which gave her the opportunity to display her acting-ability. Paradoxically, the fourth, for all its disappointments, brought her great critical recognition and the Academy Award for Best Actress.

While Paul was having his first unhappy brush with Hollywood, Joanne was working on *Count Three And Pray*, released in 1955, a maudlin Western in which the delinquent and gun-slinging Joanne was reformed by her co-star, Van Heflin. Her second picture, *A Kiss Before Dying* (1956), was withdrawn for a while after its advertising campaign provoked censorship. The film was based on Ira Levin's bestseller, and Joanne, playing Robert Wagner's murder-victim, disappeared with a lingering scream after twenty minutes or so. This must be one of the most spectacular exits in movie-history. Wagner, intent on marrying Joanne for her money, has ruined his plans by making her pregnant — a state that will surely cause her father to disinherit her. Ostensibly to marry her, Wagner takes her to the civic building, lures her up on to the roof by a ruse and while they are there tips her over the edge. She leaves the picture to a long, horrified gasp from the audience. Neverthe-less, the impression Joanne had created also lingered, though Fox were uneasy about what to do with her next. If they were not already aware of the fact, she was to prove conclusively that she could act, but star-quality was more (or less) than acting-ability, and their new Miss Woodward was proving fastidious about her scripts. To her credit, she could not stifle even for Hollywood that fierce intelligence.

For both Paul and Joanne, 1957 was to be a critical and momentous year and perhaps the only one in which her career showed signs of overtaking his.

Puzzlingly, in view of his determination to seek better pictures, Paul returned to Warners for *The Helen Morgan Story* (also known as *Both Ends Of The Candle*), which, though it was directed by the renowned (and hated — by actors) Michael Curtiz, had no fewer than four names on its screenplay and had been kicking around the studio for fifteen years — a property on which, according to rumour, twenty or more writers had exercised their skills. Not surprisingly, it turned out to be a poor film and, as biography, unfaithful to the life of the late singer who was its subject.

When Paul began working early in 1957, he clearly had mixed feelings if not about the picture then about his return to Warners, for he sent to Jack Warner a picture of himself leav-ing a walk-in refrigerator, with the caption: 'Paul Newman, who was kept in the deep-freeze for two years because of *The*

Silver Chalice, has at last been thawed out by Warner Brothers to play the cold-hearted gangster in *The Helen Morgan Story*.' In similar ambivalent mood, he presented both producer and director of the picture with whips, exhorting the men to use them if he became difficult.

But if his role was conventional, the sort of thing for which Cagney, Bogart and other Warner players had established a tradition and a pattern, Paul turned his part as Larry Maddux, a prohibition hoodlum and bootlegger, into a three-dimensional portrayal that was superior to its context. Despite the film's sentimentality and dramatics, Paul made his character credible, so that it seemed possible, if not likely, that Helen Morgan (Ann Blyth in the *truly* impossible role) should love this man who, though he cared for her in his way, so frequently abused her. Even so, for all Paul's undoubted sex-appeal, *The Helen Morgan Story* was not the sort of film to advance a career at the critical stage when it might easily have slipped backwards.

Nor, unfortunately and unjustly, was *Until They Sail*, which Paul began on loan-out to MGM (his third picture with them) the day following completion of *The Helen Morgan Story*. This was also the star's second picture with the director Robert Wise, who had served him so well on *Somebody Up There Likes Me*, and by one of the coincidences that punctuate careers like Paul's, a co-star in the same picture was Piper Laurie, who was to share top billing with him in his first great critical success, *The Hustler*.

Until They Sail is a drama about four sisters involved with American soldiers stationed in New Zealand during World War II, and it was written by Robert Anderson, adapting one of James Michener's *Return To Paradise* stories. The year before, 1956, MGM had made *Tea And Sympathy*, directed by Vincente Minnelli, which had also been written by Anderson, adapting his own successful play. Both films reveal an unusual awareness of female psychology, and the sympathetic male roles are far removed from masculine stereotypes. *Until They Sail* is a much underrated work that is progressively flawed only in its later stages, but throughout, Paul's portrait of an emotional casualty who seeks insulation in the bottle is noteworthy. Wary of wartime-romance, he struggles against falling in love with Barbara Leslie Forbes (Jean Simmons), and his performance is a telling one that holds its own against fine acting from Simmons, Piper Laurie and Charles Drake in another of the male leads. The character Paul plays, Captain Jack Harding, is cynical, disillusioned and withdrawn — another loner and introvert, like Ed Hall Jr in *The Rack*. In both pictures, Paul has all the allure of a star, and this trend of his early roles is a blow to those theorists who insist that stardom is a phenomenon that occurs when a great personality and his screen persona exactly coincide. Newman the man may be fond of seclusion and privacy, but the gregarious husband and father, with his well developed sense of fun, is markedly different from Ed Hall or Jack Harding.

Hall and Harding, it might be added, were roles sufficiently unusual — if not unique — to provoke surprise in those who knew they were witnessing Paul Newman's emergence as a great matinée-idol and sex-symbol. Marlon Brando had begun the fifties and his own screen-career by playing, in *The Men*, a wounded soldier facing daunting problems. But the man's whole predicament stems from his physical disability, whereas Ed Hall and Jack Harding are suffering from internal injuries and metaphysical dilemmas. Such characters were something new in movie-heroes. Rocky Graziano had been a man's man, and Larry Maddux a winning heel who was not above striking Helen Morgan. But Ed Hall was lonely, defeated, a tarnished hero who shed painful tears; while Jack Harding, taking refuge in his 'hot affair with the bottle', was something of a bookworm as well as a sceptic who was slowly and with reluctance compelled to admit his love for Barbara and his growing dependence on her. At a perhaps unlikely time, two-fisted hemen, it appeared, might be going out of style, and the fact that both characters wore military uniform — often a conventional shorthand for virility — served only to emphasize the uncommon sensibility that Paul projected so persuasively in the two men without in any way weakening them.

There could be no question that women liked their new romantic star, but neither *The Helen Morgan Story* nor *Until They Sail*, strongly different from each other though they were, was the type of film to propel that star to even greater fame: the one was too synthetic and factitious and the other too quiet and refined. Paul was waiting to play another Rocky Graziano — an archetype with whom a mass-audience would instantly identify.

Meanwhile, Joanne Woodward was making the picture that was to win her the Academy Award for the Best Actress of 1957 — *The Three Faces of Eve*, based on the true story by two psychiatrists, Corbett H. Thigpen and Hervey M. Cleckley, of a woman living in Augusta, Georgia, in the early 1950s. This fascinating book was a study of one of the rarest of psychological phenomena, multiple personality, and the screenplay derived from it presented an equally rare challenge for any actress. The producer and director Nunnally Johnson, perhaps knowing that she herself had been born in Georgia and could turn on a southern accent, wanted Joanne to play the three-roles-in-one — as Eve White, a drab, depressive housewife; Eve Black, her *alter ego*, a vulgar tramp; and Jane, the emergent third personality, an attractive, wholesome woman. Fox at first refused to allow Johnson to use their young contract-player, possibly thinking the part was beyond her at that stage, but they relented after several big names such as Susan Hayward had turned it down. In the event, Johnson made a pedestrian, stiffly deferential picture — a disappointment coming from the man who had shown talent, if fitfully, in the writing of Fritz Lang's *The Woman In The Window*, as well as *The Dark Mirror* and *The Gunfighter*. Even so, Joanne's performance was nothing less than the required *tour de force*, a triumph of creative acting that utilized remarkable modulations of voice, manner, physical posture and facial expression, and though in a year in which Deborah Kerr (*Heaven Knows, Mr Allison*), Anna Magnani (*Wild Is The Wind*), Elizabeth Taylor (*Raintree County*) and Lana Turner (*Peyton Place*) had all been nominated, the new star looked a poor starter in the Academy-Award stakes, she was deservedly to take the prize.

In the same year, she made *No Down Payment* — a production that will be most readily remembered for her own fine performance. It was the second film to be directed by Martin Ritt, who had made *Edge Of The City* (also known as *A Man Is Ten Feet Tall*) the previous year, with Sidney Poitier and John Cassavetes. After this stimulating directorial début, *No*

Down Payment was conventional stuff, a study of four couples living in a Los Angeles suburban development. The film inherited its superficialities and pot-pourri of social problems from the novel from which it was adapted, but Ritt managed to impart conviction to the story — though not to its melo-dramatically outrageous climax — by drawing remarkable acting from his principals and concentrating on the telling detail that revealed character.

For Fox, *No Down Payment* served as a showcase to display its younger contract-players. Cameron Mitchell, Tony Randall, Barbara Rush, Sheree North, Pat Hingle, Jeffrey Hunter and Patricia Owen were all good in it, but Joanne simply stole the picture, endowing a conventional role with a radiant humanity. (As a footnote, it should be pointed out that Cameron Mitchell was to appear in the later career of Paul Newman with an important part in *Hombre* and that Barbara Rush, who also played in *Hombre*, co-starred with Paul in *The Young Philadelphians*.)

If Paul was by now smouldering with resentment over Warners' loan-out policy, it was hardly surprising, for their fee for his services to other studios was $75,000 per picture, while they continued to pay him his standard $1,000 a week. About his next film, however, he probably had happier feelings — personal, as well as professional. It was the movie he needed, and it was to unite him for the first time on the screen with Joanne, soon to be his wife, for it started shooting in late 1957, when the Newmans' divorce was being finalized, Jackie having made her decision.

Before the main body of the unit arrived to begin working on *The Long Hot Summer* in Clinton, Mississippi, Paul pre-pared himself in typically serious fashion by spending three days in the town to drink in its atmosphere and, more impor-tantly, to study the speech and manners of its inhabitants. The authenticity of his performance revealed how worthwhile that prelude had been.

In her second picture directed by Martin Ritt, Joanne had rather more competition than in *No Down Payment* and rather less opportunity. The film is fundamentally an actors' piece that also shows how sensitively Ritt can handle an inti-mate colloquy involving two people, how well he can fuse disparate elements into a satisfying whole. Critics, though not moviegoers, were bothered by the adaptation from material in William Faulkner by Irving Ravetch and Harriet Frank Jr. (The sources are two short stories, 'Barn Burning' and 'Spotted Horses', and bits from 'The Hamlet', Books One and Two.) Despite the critics, the diversification of moods is enjoyable, and it would indeed be sad if movies were made subject to a 'doctrine of affects' as the music of Bach was, rooted in a convention demanding uniformity of emotion. Shifting moods are not the flaw in *The Long Hot Summer*, but it *is* weakened by a lack of thematic unity as interest is led from one character or set of characters to another, so that it is difficult to discern the picture's true focus of attention.

The screenplay tells of Ben Quick's ruthless climb to success and of the attempt by Will Varner, town-boss of Frenchman's Bend, to make out of the potentially dangerous Ben not simply an ally but also a son-in-law. However, Clara, Varner's daughter, is reluctant to become the wife of this seemingly boorish suitor, and Jody, Varner's son, jealous and neglected, locks the old man in the barn and sets fire to it. All ends well. Varner is delighted at his son's gumption, restoring him to his rightful place in his affections, and Clara, perceiving vulnerability beneath his brash sexuality, at last accepts Ben Quick.

Despite script weaknesses, the mixture of drama, broad comedy and exploration of character works happily, thanks to some distinguished playing. Through Ritt's intelligent direction, the relationships between the two young couples emerge touchingly, never more effectively than in some excellent bedroom-scenes between Jody and his wife, Eula (Tony Franciosa and Lee Remick). The sexual confidence and calculated charm of Ben (Paul) comes over well, and as Clara, Joanne once again turns a somewhat conventional role into a truly striking portrait. For good measure, Orson Welles (as Varner, a 'big daddy' figure strongly similar to the one who is Paul's father in the later *Cat On A Hot Tin Roof*), Angela Lansbury (his mistress) and Richard Anderson all appear at their unique best.

Tony Franciosa is excellent, too, in a role that is not exactly enviable — a half comic, half pathetic mixture of good intentions and ineptitude. As Jody, he triggers off the events of the

Paul Newman: superstar

With Diahann Carroll, Sidney Poitier and Joanne Woodward in
Paris Blues (1961)

Marital friction on screen: Paul and Joanne in *From the Terrace*
(1960)

(*top left*) As the incendiary Ben Quick in *The Long Hot Summer* (1958)

(*top right*) With Lita Milan in *The Left-Handed Gun* (1958)

Kitty Fremont (Eva Marie Saint) saves Ari Ben Canaan's life in *Exodus* (1960)

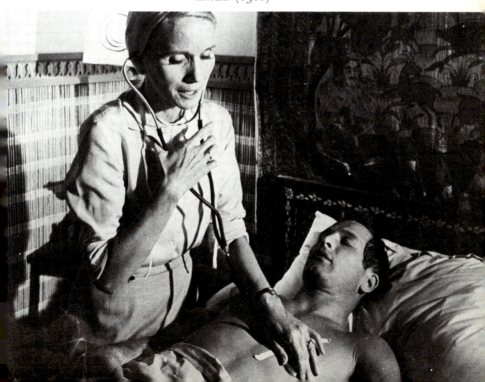

As Fast Eddie Felson in *The Hustler* (1961)

With Piper Laurie in *The Hustler*

With Brandon de Wilde during the shooting of *Hud* (1963)

Paul and Joanne display premarital friction in *A New Kind of Love*
(1963)

Masquerading as a pensive priest in *Lady L* (1965)

Sharing a joke with director Peter Ustinov during the making of *Lady L*

(*top left*) On set as *Harper*
(1966)

(*top right*) With rarely seen
moustache at Stratford-
upon-Avon, 1969

(*left*) Professional advice:
Paul and Judi Dench

drama by letting a tenant-farm to Ben Quick while Varner is in hospital — unaware of Quick's reputation for settling grudges by burning down barns. Some of Franciosa's dialogue ('Am I your son or ain't I? You ain't never been a poppa to me.') is hard to handle, and the actor copes astonishingly well with it, but the casting of Paul Newman in the dominant, showy part of Quick almost ensures that Franciosa is overlooked.

In only her second film, Lee Remick, who was then in her early twenties, makes a vivid impression in the small but important role of Eula. Nearly two decades later, she was to tell the author: 'My memories of working with both Paul and Joanne (and Martin Ritt) are clouded by the fact that I was very new to films at that time and completely *terrified* of everyone! They were all very good to me, and I was totally in awe of them!'

Ben Quick was the character for which Paul's career had been waiting since *Somebody Up There Likes Me* — a colourful extrovert, sneering daredevil and superbly attractive lover. The part, however, is more appealing and less one-dimensional than it might sound from that capsule description. The star's charm ensures that we are never quite alienated by his sometimes antisocial or threatening behaviour, and in a scene with Clara near the end of the picture, this sardonic upstart, his eyes filling with tears, allows a glimpse of the tenderness beneath his tough shell in the type of revelation that Paul, even if he did not pioneer it, was coming to specialize in.

Charm, his greatest asset as a star, was to be his biggest handicap as a performer, but its problems lay in the future. Charm can be a dangerous quality for an actor. When you have it, you have to use it; and sometimes when you think you are not using it, it creeps out anyway. It is like a fire that may be damped down but can never be extinguished.

There is no conclusive evidence on whether being in love helps actors to play lovers on stage or screen, but it did not observably inhibit Paul and Joanne in *The Long Hot Summer*. On the contrary, they perform together with a rapport that, given their deepening offscreen relationship, is readily understandable.

To sum up, the picture is hard to dislike and its star hard to resist. He proves that he can dominate a production, and his charm finds its easy justification in the need both to persuade audiences that the hustler he is playing really could carry off his feats and to prevent their finding him repellently ruthless. Paul's first great box-office success had yet to arrive, but *The Long Hot Summer* did good business.

Statistically, it was a significant film — the first of three important screenplays by Ravetch and Frank that punctuated Paul's career; the first of seven occasions on which he has co-starred with Joanne; and the beginning of a fruitful six-picture association with director Martin Ritt.

Most obviously because that was the year in which Paul and Joanne were wed, 1958 was a year to remember. But it was also remarkable for the quickening tempo of Paul's career (no fewer than four of his films were released) and for the honours, almost like wedding-gifts, that came to the couple. Joanne of course received her Academy Award, but Paul was the only American to win that year at the Cannes Film Festival, where he was named Best Actor for *The Long Hot Summer*.

1958 began, however, with another joint-performance. On 16th January, Paul and Joanne co-starred in a Playhouse 90 production *The 80-Yard Run*, usually cited as the star's best work in television. He is cast as a college football-hero who marries the campus-belle (Joanne). In later life, the disparity in their fortunes tugs them inexorably in opposite directions. She has a successful job with a fashion-magazine, but in the years of the Depression he is unemployed, his assurance being eroded as his wife's is strengthened. In self-pity and despair, he contemplates what was, in retrospect, the climax of his life — the 80-yard run of the title. The drama lasted ninety minutes and had been adapted by David Shaw from a short story by his brother, Irwin Shaw. The *New York Times* found it 'absorbing' and described the acting of the principals as 'excellent'.

Two weeks later, on 29th January, Paul and Joanne were married at the Hotel El Rancho Vegas in Las Vegas. To husband and wife, their new status was all but incredible — a matter at first for deep relief rather than joy. At last, the many months of strain were over. They went straight to New York and thence to a honeymoon in Europe. In February, they were at the Connaught in London, a city that they fell in love with, protected at that time by their comparative lack of fame. Staying overnight at inns they came across more or less casually, they toured as far as Scotland, and in future years, they were to refresh their happy memories with occasional and little publicized visits to Great Britain.

In Hollywood, that tiny village where, as Melville Shavelson has said, 'rumours carry more weight than fact', the marriage had been predicted for some time. For once, though, the columnists were right, but by the time the marriage at last became fact, Paul had had enough of the Press, who had scarcely been kind to him critically or, perhaps more importantly, considerate during the period of the break-up of his first partnership. The effects were long-lasting. If the experience implied being quoted in print, the star was to refuse to be interviewed. Furthermore, he has an abiding reluctance to answering personal questions, though he is quite ready to discuss his acting during the rare interviews to which he consents, just as he will also talk about his political activities. Newman the man remains private property, and perhaps the gentleman and ladies of the Press — collectively, if not individually — have only themselves to blame. (Journalistic garbage has an ironic tendency to make its subject sound ridiculous instead of its author.)

Still, though the Press might be avoided, its interest could not thereby be dissipated — indeed, if anything, the Newmans' urge for privacy heightened the curiosity of the fourth estate. And it *was* a marriage to fire the imagination — the union of a golden couple who by all appearances were about to conquer the world. Of course, all such romantic notions are capable of inversion, and there were — and still are — columnists who, remembering that golden lads and girls must come to dust, were waiting impatiently for signs that the marriage might be unstable. It was to prove a long wait — twenty years (to date) not of undiluted bliss but of willed reciprocity and the tenacity and flexibility that are at least as important as love.

They were not children. Paul's first marriage had taught him something, if only about human fallibility, and Joanne was twenty-eight, an advanced age, by the standards of her southern background, at which to marry. Furthermore, she once pointed out that she became engaged three times after she first met Paul Newman. (Gore Vidal and James Costigan were two of the men.) She had not been exactly hasty or impetuous in her commitment. Thus neither of the partners began their new life with the unblurred expectations of intact teenagers, and their comparative maturity was to be needed from the start, for Joanne was not to gain a ready acceptance from her husband's three children. Then there were the problems of two careers.

No more consistent than other men or women, Joanne has varied in her statements over the years about the relative importance of her marriage and her acting. On the one hand, she has talked about putting Paul's career first and sacrificing her own ambitions; on the other, she (and even more vehemently Paul himself) tends to deny that she ever relinquished her aspirations in acting, insisting that a lack of good scripts rather than her marriage has kept her inactive. Similarly, that marriage itself has occasionally been described in terms that suggest a changing and decidedly not sterile relationship. The ideal of being constantly together appears with the passing of time to have been replaced by a realization of the deep human need for variety and change, and in later life the Newmans have spent approximately half the year apart. But if their concept of marriage has altered, intimacy is not to be measured by the calendar and though they may not be persistently together, there is a sense of the continuing evolution of a relationship that has had its frictions and developed just as surely through them as through the happy times.

Nevertheless, in the late fifties and early sixties, the Newmans were to celebrate their new status through shared professional involvement, though Paul was first to make two more films solo.

The newly-weds returned to Hollywood, but their aversion to the *mores* and manners of the film-colony was one of the many ways in which they were united. If Hollywood was of necessity their base for work, their true home was to be in Connecticut — a converted coaching-house, dating back to 1780, with three acres of apple-orchard and a trout-stream.

Once they and the children of their marriage had settled there, they tried — insofar as it was possible — to live a 'normal' life and to fit quietly into the local community. If, in the years that followed, all this unspectacular living was to sound incongruously parochial or rural for two whom the unwary might have considered sophisticated urbanites, the Newmans had selected their Connecticut retreat precisely to escape what they believed to be the *true* parochialism of Hollywood — that inbred microcosm, preoccupied with 'the business' and refusing to lift its eyes to wider horizons. This deliberate attitude was seen by some as shunning if not actually biting the hand that fed them, and it did little for the Newmans' popularity within the tiny colony.

Their considered choice of a lifestyle should be related to the approaches of both husband and wife to their shared craft. Joanne may be the intuitive one, but Paul has always been a great observer of ordinary folk, from whom he derives many of the ideas that he incorporates into his roles. Actors who constantly watch and are in the company of other actors are in grave danger of becoming stale, of 'cribbing' from their contemporaries instead of evolving their own, fresh conception of a part; and while the Newmans number other actors (for example, Robert Wagner and Natalie Wood) among their friends, their social circle takes in many people from outside the world of films, including businessmen, politicians and authors. Part of the reason why London had appealed instantly to them on their honeymoon was that they sensed that actors in the capital were less inclined to lead the convoluted, self-regarding existence that the Newmans were familiar with elsewhere.

5

Scaling the Heights

Paul returned to Warners for his first Western, and like the subsequent examples of the genre in which he has starred, it was far from traditional or conventional. *The Left-Handed Gun* was produced by Fred Coe and directed by Arthur Penn, both of them from television. Penn's first film had a screenplay by Leslie Stevens based on Gore Vidal's teleplay, *The Death Of Billy The Kid*, and the picture is consistently arresting but not arrestingly consistent — either in style or content. In the three years from 1956 to 1959, Paul was to get much out of his actor's system. Notably, the twitches, hesitations and hand-gestures that some critics had pounced upon in his early performances began to give way to a less cluttered manner. These were at their most pronounced, however, under Arthur Penn's direction, and *The Left-Handed Gun* is crammed with artificial excesses, some of them the star's. Though, with the passing of the years and the consolidation of Penn's reputation, it has become a cult-movie, critics and audiences were right to feel confused by it: while individual scenes may be effective, it fails to hang together stylistically, in terms of character or in the writing, which prompts Paul to play Billy as a mixed-up, not-too-bright kid. Nevertheless, among the baroque extravagances, there are touches of freshness and originality, not least in the sequence during which Billy, grieving over the death of his protector, learns the identities of the man's four murderers, whom he will pursue and kill. In childish glee, a sudden change of mood, Paul marches up and down with a broom — one of the best moments in a performance that is never less than interesting.

The Left-Handed Gun had a modest budget and a modest (twenty-three days) shooting-schedule and received the kind of notices usually described as 'mixed' (George Kaufman wittily defined them as 'good and rotten'). In a published study of Penn's work, one of the most specious and turgid chapters is devoted to the picture, and admirers of the director's movies have bemoaned the fact that Penn and Newman have never worked together again. Years afterwards, however, Paul said, 'I still don't like the film. It's artificial.' Many would agree with the star's judgement, but *The Left-Handed Gun*, for all its inequalities, exerts a grudging fascination, and Paul's acting repays observation if only because he is never more eloquent in the role of Billy than when he is without words. Though the interpretation seems ultimately outside his control, his use of his eyes, face and body speaks tellingly for the inarticulate character he is playing.

It was ironic that Paul's next picture, *Cat On A Hot Tin Roof*, made for MGM, was to bring him his first Academy Award nomination, for although he performs in it about as well as could be expected, given such a context, the film is something of a shambles. Deriving from the play by Tennessee Williams, it was directed and co-written (with James Poe) by Richard Brooks, who, in an earlier adaptation, had already turned *The Brothers Karamazov* into a travesty and was to acquire a reputation for fatally diluting literary and dramatic masterpieces by the time he had also filmed Williams's *Sweet Bird Of Youth* and Sinclair Lewis's *Elmer Gantry* in the sixties. In fairness to Brooks, however, it should be admitted that, though *Elmer Gantry* is far from being Lewis's novel, it is an impressive, thoughtful film, while at least some of the weaknesses to be found in *Cat On A Hot Tin Roof* are the result of sidestepping the censorship difficulties that prevailed at the time of its making.

The drama begins with the return of Big Daddy (Burl Ives), a rich Southerner, to his plantation after a spell in hospital, where, unknown to him, terminal cancer has been diagnosed. His family are waiting to celebrate his sixty-fifth birthday, but his younger son Brick (Paul), using as an excuse the broken ankle he has acquired during a drunken outing on the athletics field, keeps to his bedroom, drinking heavily and deflecting the advances of his beautiful wife Maggie (Elizabeth Taylor), with whom he has sworn never to sleep again. His absence gives his brother Gooper (Jack Carson) and his wife Mae (Madeleine Sherwood) the chance to scheme to take over all Brick's share in the inheritance. They join Big Mama (Judith Anderson), Big Daddy's wife, in a conspiracy to keep from the old man the truth about his physical condition. Knowing exactly what is going on, Maggie fights to protect Brick's interests, and Big Daddy and Brick, the former enraged by his son's deliberately maintained distance, have a row about his behaviour and his tardiness in becoming a father. Past events are uncovered, notably the death of Skipper, Brick's best friend, for whose suicide he blames Maggie, since he believes she had an affair with Skipper. But Brick admits that he failed to help his friend 'in the hour of his need' when Skipper telephoned him just before ending it all. Truth and revelation are in the air, and Brick, emotional at being forced to confess his guilt, inadvertently blurts out the truth about Big Daddy's medical check-up. Severe pain begins to bite into Big Daddy, and as a climax to the drama, father and son are at last reconciled, each facing up to his own harsh reality. Aware that Brick's attitude to her is softening, Maggie announces to the assembled family that her birthday present to Big Daddy is her own pregnancy. With the implication that it will rapidly become truth, Brick backs up her lie.

If Brooks expected his audience to have seen the play before they watched the film, in which Brick's sense of guilt is virtually opaque, he was asking too much. For those without previous knowledge of the Tennessee Williams original, however, the film's central episode becomes vague and puzzling, failing to explain satisfactorily an obscure emotional hang-up in the character of Brick. Williams, of course, *had* explained and justified it in his play, in which Brick accuses Maggie of breaking up a deep friendship between him and Skipper, with the result that Skipper went to pieces fast and died an alcoholic. Big Daddy, though, compels Brick to recognize that the nature of that friendship had been homosexual. The motivation for Brick's conduct is therefore much stronger and more specific in the play.

To an extent, one could sympathize with Brooks. In order to get the property on to the screen at all, the homosexual key to Brick's character provided by Williams had to be discarded. But the film was flawed by more than this revision. Brooks and Poe emasculated the author's language, important scenes lacked conviction and failed to fit into the new conception, and the direction, though it scarcely avoided melodrama, lacked drive.

All this blurring of intentions might have bothered the perceptive, but it did not deter audiences, who gave Paul his first great box-office success. And why not? The public were being offered two great sex-symbols — Newman and Elizabeth Taylor. He looked marvellous, and his torso, whether he liked it or not, was on display, while Elizabeth Taylor spent much of the film in a slip that suggested, if it did not reveal, her luscious form, which was not concealed overmuch, either, by glamorous dresses with spectacular *décolletage*. Furthermore, there was the piquant sight of the virile and athletic Paul Newman, the pin-up of an increasing number of women the world over, flat on his back and resisting the advances of Miss Taylor, undoubted sex-queen of that era and the woman most males in the audience, unlike Brick, would have voted the one they would Most Like To Be Pursued By. It was a stimulating juxtaposition.

On a more sober level, it should be said that Paul gave a sound performance. For most of the picture, he is self-contained, withdrawn, contemptuously tranquil in the face of Taylor's passionate outbursts, thus setting up a valuable contrast. But the actor who feared to 'let go' is splendidly intense and emotional in his key-scene with Burl Ives, bringing off a coup rather like his achievement in the father-son reconciliation of *The Rack*. Even so, he is perhaps at his best when he is at his most uncommunicative, holding himself stiffly, hanging on to his almost symbolic crutch and refusing to face those who harangue him.

Ben Gazzara had played the original Brick on Broadway in 1955, and it is easy to imagine how his performance might have differed from Paul's — more smouldering and sardonic, perhaps. Both actors, curiously enough, could easily be considered too strong for the role. However, Williams himself, though he reportedly disliked the picture, admired Paul as Brick.

Even if she had not been the first nomination, Elizabeth Taylor was in some ways a good choice for Maggie the Cat. She certainly embodied the sensuality of the character, and she managed, too, to convey tenderness in the midst of her sturdy support for Brick. Encouraged by her husband Mike

Todd and having already gained an Academy Award nomination for *Raintree County*, she sought to extend her range, and despite unnerving conditions that will be explained later, her acting in *Cat On A Hot Tin Roof*, if it could scarcely be compared with that of Barbara Bel Geddes as the original Maggie, won her new respect. (Grace Kelly had been slated for the picture, but she took up a new life in Monaco long before it began shooting. Another who backed out was George Cukor, who was once rumoured as director before MGM's Dore Schary handed over the property to Richard Brooks.)

Among the rest of the cast, Judith Anderson is excellent, and Burl Ives, who created the part originally, begins monotonously as Big Daddy and ends with great force and conviction. Perhaps best of all, however, are Madeleine Sherwood (also in the Broadway production) and Jack Carson, who make the most of their straightforward roles.

The drama of *Cat On A Hot Tin Roof* was not to be merely in the film. Shooting began on 12th March. A week or so later, Mike Todd was to be guest of honour at a Friars Testimonial Dinner at the Waldorf-Astoria in New York, and on the night of 21st March, in torrential rain, he took off from Southern California in his twin-engined Lockheed Lodestar that he had called 'The Lucky Liz'. Early the following morning, the plane crashed in the Zuni Mountains of New Mexico, killing Todd together with his pilot and co-pilot.

For Elizabeth Taylor, it was a time of overwhelming grief, but after the funeral, though she was still not fit to resume work, she watched on television the Academy Awards ceremony at which she should have been a presenter. In the event of her winning as Best Actress for *Raintree County*, Jennifer Jones would accept for her. Ironically, the winner, for *The Three Faces Of Eve*, turned out to be Joanne Woodward. Later, at the ball following the ceremony, Joanne was presented with a box of white orchids while she and Paul were celebrating her success. The accompanying card read: 'I am so happy for you. Elizabeth Taylor Todd and Mike, too.'

On 14th April, Taylor returned to the set of *Cat On A Hot Tin Roof*, and she was guided and helped through that difficult period by Paul and Richard Brooks. Her eventual nomination for yet another Academy Award had the extra distinction of being earned bravely during the time of her immediate bereavement.

As for the picture itself, artistic defects did not prevent commercial triumph: *Cat On A Hot Tin Roof* was not only the top moneymaker of 1958 but also MGM's tenth biggest grosser up to that time.

Even if Paul had been close to another's tragedy during the making of his latest film, life must have seemed more than promising for him, especially when the Newmans found the script that would reunite them on film. Furthermore, for both Paul and Joanne, it would be a change of pace — a chance to explore their lighter gifts in farce.

In the event, the picture turned out to be a disaster.

On paper, *Rally 'Round The Flag, Boys* had no doubt looked good. The novel on which it was based had been written by Max Shulman, who had also written — among other novels, short stories, plays and screenplays — *Barefoot Boy With Cheek*, which was a huge success and became a Broadway musical; *The Tender Trap* (with Robert Paul Smith), a Broadway hit and movie-success for Sinatra and Debbie Reynolds; and *The Many Loves Of Dobie Gillis*, which became a very funny movie, again starring Debbie Reynolds. Having spent memorable hours in Shulman's company, the author can testify that he is among the wittiest of men. The screenplay for *Rally 'Round The Flag, Boys* was written by Leo McCarey and Claude Binyon, the second of whom, besides being an experienced director, was the author of the screenplays for *You Can't Run Away From It*, *North To Alaska* and *Kisses For My President*. As for Leo McCarey, who could have asked for a better director? This was the man who had paired Stan Laurel and Oliver Hardy, had directed some of their greatest shorts such as *From Soup To Nuts* and had also directed one of the classic film-comedies, *The Awful Truth* — besides such sure-fire commercial successes as *Going My Way*.

But the truth was that though the original novel of *Rally 'Round The Flag, Boys* had been amusing, the screenplay was flat and uninventive, and even if he had a distinguished career dating back to the twenties, there had always been signs that McCarey, for all the warmth and brilliance of his comedy at its best, was an uneven director who was capable of unnervingly poor judgement. *Rally 'Round The Flag, Boys*, near the end of that career, was to be one of his off-days, even though one commentator has since praised him for casting Paul Newman as Joan Collins's straight man.

The plot scarcely bears recounting, but concerns the inhabitants of Putnam's Landing, Connecticut, who are thrown into consternation by the news that the town has been chosen as the secret site for a missile-base. Grace Bannerman (Joanne) sends her husband Harry (Paul) to Washington to argue the case with the Pentagon. While Harry is being pursued by Angela (Joan Collins), a bored and predatory neighbour, Grace discovers the two of them in her husband's hotel-room. The circumstances, though innocent, look otherwise. As a result of the ensuing quarrel, Harry joins the other side, and the military give him the job of persuading his fellow-townsfolk to accept the secret project. Grace stages a town-pageant, under cover of which the military are attacked. In the midst of the mêlée, the Bannermans, reconciled, accidentally fire the missile, which vanishes into space along with the base-commander, the boorish Captain Hoxie (Jack Carson).

Not surprisingly, the film did poor business, and there were reviewers who leapt at the chance to blame the stars for its fiasco. This attitude was nonetheless reprehensible for being understandable, for professionals and alleged specialists should have been aware that when most movies either fail or succeed, the venture is essentially collaborative. In her book *The Verdict*, Hildegard Knef, speaking of herself in the third person, writes perceptively of the influences at work in commercial moviemaking:

> She had come to realise that the so-called film-star's lot is an infantile and precarious one, since critics and public alike are apt to make him responsible for the final product; the ugly truth is that whatever a star's box-office standing and however much he may exercise his power during the making of the picture, there is a whole battalion of other participants lurking in the background just waiting to gum up the works, namely, author, producer, director, editor, and, last but by no means least, distributor. On rare occasions the finished article will turn out as good as, perhaps even better than, the star expected it to, but here again, it's

through no fault of his. Whatever the outcome, the success or failure of the movie will be automatically linked with the name above the title, the star carried the day or carried the can, earned deserved fame or undeserved blame.

Though Paul Newman and Joanne Woodward deserved no blame (except, arguably, for their choice of property), they were certainly to 'carry the can' for *Rally 'Round The Flag, Boys*. Unjustly, the critics asserted that Paul had no flair for comedy. Similarly, they indicted Joanne, who had already shown convincing touches of humour in both *No Down Payment* and *The Three Faces Of Eve* and was to be praised by Pauline Kael for 'a wide streak of humour about herself that you sense and respond to'. For the discerning, the film revealed not only what they probably already knew — that Paul possessed charm that, just as it had secured sympathy for Billy the Kid, enabled him to bestow a — spurious — coherence on the otherwise inscrutable Brick in *Cat On A Hot Tin Roof*; but also that he had a well developed sense of fun. It is to be observed, splendidly, in an almost silent sequence of *Rally 'Round The Flag, Boys* in which Paul battles his way to the bar in the crowded club-car of a commuters' train. So hemmed in by elbows that he cannot drink (and his miming here is excellent), he at last finds a relatively free space behind a door and raises his glass to his lips. At that moment, the door flies open and the hard-won glass is dashed from his hand. Gestures and facial expressions combine to hilarious effect in this sequence, and to show that Paul's comedic gifts are no fluke, they are again effectively demonstrated in *Exodus* and *Harper*. (Perhaps it is not without significance that neither of these pictures could by any stretch of definition be called a comedy.) In *Exodus*, there is a scene in which Paul impersonates a British officer, though he is himself a Jew. A fellow-officer, Peter Lawford, claims that he has an unerring intuition that enables him to detect Jews. With great relish that is both conveyed to and reciprocated by audiences, Paul pretends that he has something in his eye — and eyes, according to Lawford, are the surest guide to Jewishness — and has Lawford remove it. Again, in *Harper*, Paul, accompanied by Robert Wagner, stumbles across a locked door that blocks his investigation.

Enchanted by being in the company of a private-eye, Wagner wistfully evinces his desire to barge the door open with his shoulder. Magnanimous, Paul allows him the privilege of trying, and Wagner predictably ends up with a badly bruised shoulder while the door remains intact. Here, Paul's gift for parody, his sense that traditional gestures are ludicrous and doomed to failure, come across in his expressions of wry amusement. It is a shame that such gifts have not been better used.

As if doubly to sour Newman's experience, *Rally 'Round The Flag, Boys* had again been made on loan-out — this time to Fox. Partly in reaction, he wanted to get back to the stage. Not unlike other actors before him — Errol Flynn, for example — but with greater conviction, he believed that acting in films was too 'easy', too protected and that the vulnerability of live performance was at once salutary and stimulating. Furthermore, moviemaking, for all its triumphs, had had failure and disappointments, whereas on Broadway he had known nothing but success. However, Warners' price for leave of absence had to be paid, and it proved to be a picture called *The Young Philadelphians* (also known as *The City Jungle*).

Thus, in 1959, he found himself playing Tony Judson Lawrence in an adaptation by James Gunn from Richard Powell's novel *The Philadelphian*. Tony is the illegitimate son of a woman whose husband deserts her on her wedding-night after she has married into the Philadelphia aristocracy. Unaware of the circumstances of his birth, Tony is raised as an aristocratic but impoverished Lawrence instead of as the son of Mike Flanagan, a contractor. In his twenties, Tony ambitiously pursues a law-career, so losing his chance to marry Joan Dickinson (Barbara Rush). With money and security as his only goals, Tony now finds his progress interrupted by the Korean War, which also makes Joan a widow and therefore available again. Tony begins to flourish as a specialist in tax-law (tax-evasion might be a more accurate term), but when his alcoholic ex-college-chum Chet Gwynne (Robert Vaughn) is indicted for the murder of his guardian, Tony decides to defend him. Tony's mother is warned that if he does so, the circumstances of his birth will be disclosed, but Tony scorns the threat, successfully defends Chet by proving that his guardian committed suicide, and becomes reconciled with Joan, who had previously despaired over his opportunism.

The film's director, Vincent Sherman, was a Warners veteran who had made a number of Bette Davis and Joan Crawford movies, with which *The Young Philadelphians* has strong affinities. But if the work is decidedly soap-opera, it is also well paced and insidiously persuasive. The climactic trial is a poor, unconvincing affair; even the villains of the piece turn soft-hearted in the end; and Tony's political aspirations, which will mean foregoing a comfortable niche in society, inexplicably and limply peter out as if someone had forgotten that they were ever mentioned in the script.

In this, the last film of the second segment of Paul Newman's Hollywood career, his charm and sex-appeal distort for perhaps the first time, with the result that it becomes hard to realize what Barbara Rush finds so hurtful and despicable, since Paul's shoddy aims and actions are a part of one so personable and attractive. Though it has sometimes been suggested that Paul was observably 'walking through' to work out his Warner contract, his performance is generally a good one — too good. In the end, having striven hard and sacrificed much, Tony Lawrence wins both the big law-case and Barbara Rush, with whom he has long been in love. For all its surface-conviction, the story is hard to believe, its 'message' far from pure, but given the star's grace and allure, the ending is easy to accept, the more so as it contains an ingredient of proven effectiveness — the hasty and last-minute renunciation of materialistic desires. After all, isn't it a great American dream to get the girl *and* the money? (And quite a trick to pull it off when you have just foresworn worldly ambition: it is hard to see how Tony's success as a trial-lawyer, which has made him no enemies, can do him anything but good. If Tony can go on — as he clearly can — as a wealthy socialite, the whole point of his decision to defend Chet is lost.)

Pictures engaged in such sleight-of-hand need canny direction and seductive acting, and *The Young Philadelphians* has both. As well as Paul, Barbara Rush, a born tragedienne who has seldom found suitable roles, is outstandingly good in a part that allows her a great deal of heartbreak and stoicism. Robert Vaughn, subtly conveying weakness and despair ('You don't think I drink this stuff because I like it, do you?'), comes near to stealing all the scenes in which he appears, and the ever-reliable Brian Keith scores heavily as Tony's real father. Yet as a social climber, Paul unquestionably has the plum-role — which is not always the same as the star-role. It enables him to exhibit impeccable manners, shrewd deference and a sure instinct for the niceties of business-etiquette — and so attractively that their effect would have been fatal to serious moral intentions, had the film possessed any.

As a footnote to the casting of *The Young Philadelphians*, it might be added that it contains one of those allocations of roles that become unintentionally entertaining with the passage of time. Playing the socialite who at the beginning of the picture proves impotent on his wedding-night and subsequently commits suicide is Adam West, later to move on to fame as television's omnipotent Batman.

While her husband kept busy, Joanne had hardly been idle, and her career continued with two interesting, if not exactly successful, pictures, *The Sound And The Fury* and *The Fugitive Kind*. In the first, she was what David Shipman has wittily and perceptively dubbed 'a Deep South Jane Eyre', playing Quentin, the young ward of Jason Compson (Yul Brynner). This was Martin Ritt's second trip south and in the company of the same writing-team, Ravetch and Frank, who had worked on *The Long Hot Summer*. Faulkner country again: crumbling plantation-house; faded southern belle (Margaret Leighton) and her rebellious daughter whom she had abandoned at birth (Joanne); fragmented, not to say degenerate, family held together by the grim Jason, a member by adoption who is determined to enhance its status. Resenting his authority, Quentin takes the money her mother has sent her periodically during her abandonment, and tries to run away with a carnival roustabout. Jason pursues them, and when he proves that the man is interested not in her but in her money, Quentin realizes that her feelings towards Jason are significantly changing.

At 115 minutes, *The Sound And The Fury* is a long, hard slog, with ill-conceived characters and meandering concerns. Though her part is written scarcely a cut above the feeblest women's fiction, Joanne's performance illuminates the film and is full of sensitivity and intelligence. That said, the picture must be counted a failure, despite acting that is often better than the material deserves. The pace is slow, and the obscurely created role of Jason has its opacity augmented by the playing of Yul Brynner, labouring under the handicaps of a supposedly southern accent and a hennaed wig. This lacuna at the heart of the drama is a pity, because the plot-ramifications are considerable, and had Brynner been able to shed light on Jason's moods, his motives and his agony, the feat might have imposed some badly needed unity on the piece.

With *The Fugitive Kind*, there was an unmistakable sense that Joanne, because of her origins and past performances, was in real danger of being typecast in parts requiring her to portray demented southern womanhood. As it turned out, nothing about the picture – save, perhaps, her own playing – was calculated to add lustre to her reputation. Failure and abortion marked the history of the drama, which had begun life as Tennessee Williams's *Battle Of Angels*, a play that opened and closed out of town in 1939. (The author received a Rockefeller fellowship for it.) As *Orpheus Descending* and considerably reshaped, it eventually appeared on Broadway, and it was rewritten yet again by Williams and Meade Roberts to become the film *The Fugitive Kind*. The screenplay, however, retained all the awkwardness of a youthful work, constantly revised, but lost the freshness of emotional concerns that had prompted the young dramatist to write it in the first place.

Coming from a writer of slighter reputation than Williams, the plot might have been described as an outlandish farrago. It concerns Val Xavier (Marlon Brando), a thirty-two-year-old drifter and guitarist, who has been run out of New Orleans. Arriving in a small town, he takes work in a store run by Lady Torrance (Anna Magnani), a sex-starved woman standing in for the real owner, her husband Jabe (Victor Jory), who is bed-ridden and dying of cancer. Val and Lady experience mutual attraction, but Val is also pursued by Carol Cutrere (Joanne), an alcoholic nymphomaniac and daughter of the best family in town. When Lady becomes pregnant by Val, the vengeful Jabe shoots his wife dead and sets fire to the parlour, almost holy in its significance, built by the lovers behind the store. The sheriff and hostile townsfolk arrive, and Val is driven by the force of their pressure-hoses into the inferno. When the flames subside, Carol wanders through the ruins and recovers Val's snakeskin jacket, which she has appeared to covet as much as the body of its owner.

If the events and characters thus simplified in a brief synopsis do not sound exactly like *The Aldrich Family*, *The Fugitive Kind* is certainly nothing of the sort. Giving Williams the most generous licence to toy with the myth of Orpheus, one can say only that much of the symbolism of the drama is obscure, whatever resonances it may contain for its creator. Sidney Lumet, the director, realized that the character Val— the hero, if so unconventional a piece could possibly contain anybody as conventional as a hero—faded from the story in the second half. But by that time he and everyone else were committed—not least Brando, who, though he knew well that the role of Val was too undeveloped on paper for him to do much with it, had to go ahead with *The Fugitive Kind* and take the million dollars he had been offered—the first actor to obtain such a fee. Brando's own pet-project, *One-Eyed Jacks*, had put his Pennebaker Productions deeply into the red, and he had personal obligations as well that forced him to participate in the venture, however insecure it might look. Last-minute revisions from Williams did not improve the prospect, and Lumet's direction, apparently seeking to minimize or mute the overblown language of the screenplay, was to succeed only in drawing attention to the inflated nature of the goings-on.

In the opening scene, Brando stood before a judge and looked, in his sullen detachment, like the legendary rebel-artist whom Williams had probably envisaged. But as Lumet was to point out, you could not make *Orpheus Descending* without Orpheus, and the beginning was also to be the end. Magnani tried to subdue her extravagance, her one great asset as an actress, and as a result became unintelligible. Brando played Stanley Kowalski with a lute. And Victor Jory, perhaps out of frustration, all but chewed the scenery. The whole circus added up to an artistic and commercial disaster.

Where, in the midst of all this, was Joanne Woodward?

The answer was that she was almost buried beneath her make-up, mainly the white visage of a clown, but with black eyes and a nose that bled profusely at the slightest provocation. Her great moment was when she attempted to seduce Brando in a cemetery. Although Carol Cutrere was one of Williams's most feverish creations, however, Joanne bestowed upon the character the luminosity appropriate to a symbol, and her participation had interest as a technical piece of acting.

Paul Newman's reactions to *The Fugitive Kind* have not been recorded, but he must have experienced mixed feelings at seeing his wife perform opposite Brando — the very star who, in Paul's early years, had been persistently introduced into facile comparisons that were always to Newman's disadvantage.

For Paul, 1959 was a year to remember in at least three different ways. He returned to Broadway in an impressive gesture that was really more than a gesture — rather, a re-affirmation of his belief that live performance prevented an actor from becoming lazy. A month later, on 7th April, he became a father for the fourth time when Joanne gave birth to a daughter, Elinor, the first child of their marriage. And in August, though it still had three years to run, he bought out his contract with Warners.

Paul opened in Tennessee Williams's *Sweet Bird Of Youth* on 10th March 1959, at the Martin Beck Theatre, New York, the play being directed by Elia Kazan. The production ran for forty-two weeks and 336 performances, of which Paul missed not a single one. He co-starred with Geraldine Page, and also in the cast were Rip Torn and Madeleine Sherwood — all of whom, together with Paul, would again take up their roles when Richard Brooks filmed *Sweet Bird Of Youth* for MGM in 1962.

The play, the plot of which was to be substantially changed for filming, relates how Chance Wayne (Paul) returns to his Florida hometown in the company of Alexandra Del Lago (Geraldine Page), a fading moviestar, considerably his senior, with whom he is amorously and opportunistically entangled, his hope being that she will ease his own path into the movie-business. Chance wishes to see again his former girl, Heavenly Finley (Diana Hyland), the daughter of a local political giant, Boss Finley (Sidney Blackmer). As Chance has infected Heavenly with venereal disease and made her pregnant, Boss Finley has forbidden her ever to associate with him again, but Chance is determined to talk to her. While Alexandra languishes in her hotel-room, muffling her despair over a washed-up career with booze and drugs, Sally Powers, a Hollywood columnist, calls to inform her that her latest film is a hit, ensuring her desired comeback. With an instant change of mood, she packs for Hollywood, making it clear that there is no room in her plans for Chance, who has not succeeded in seeing Heavenly, his attempts having been frustrated by Tom Finley (Rip Torn), her brother. Alexandra urges Chance to leave in order to evade Tom and his friends, who are coming to the hotel-room to castrate him, but Chance, without self-pity, tells her that he has outlived his time and refuses to go.

On Broadway, *Sweet Bird Of Youth* was a very different drama from that seen by a mass-audience on the screen — in which it was not Chance Wayne who was emasculated but Williams's words, actions and ideas. Not only did the play, with its theme of lost youth and doomed innocence, powerfully move those who saw it, but also Paul Newman and Geraldine Page gave performances of a lifetime, and Paul's magnificent acting stimulated the best reviews he had had so far. He conveyed to perfection Chance's fatalism at the end of Act Three ('Whatever happens to me's already happened'), and Robert Coleman of the *New York Daily Mirror* reported that Newman and his audience alike had tears in their eyes. His performance was a *coup de théâtre* for which, unfortunately, he was to find no equivalent in the screen-version.

In the summer, three months after *The Young Philadel-*

phians opened to mixed notices, some of which suggested —
quite unconvincingly — that its star had not been trying, Paul
terminated his unhappy association with Warners. During
his five-year spell with the studio, he had made perhaps
three films of sufficient all-round excellence to display his
talent at its best — and not one of them had been a Warner
picture. When studio and star parted company, he said that
they were at the time paying him $17,500 per film, including
the loan-outs, for each of which they picked up $75,000
for Newman's services. To buy out his contract, he paid
a sum reported to be $500,000. Enormous sum that it might
seem, its magnitude was not to worry him for long. His
next film, *From The Terrace*, was to be a big hit, adding
lustre to his status as a star of enduring popularity, and
he was thereafter able to obtain $200,000 a film.

In a sense, Paul returned to the West Coast in stages,
taking part in the shooting of *From The Terrace* by day
towards the end of *Sweet Bird Of Youth*'s run and appearing in the play at night. He left the production in January
1960, and went back to Hollywood to finish the picture.
It was an interesting way of re-immersing himself in the
movie-colony. He had walked out on it for the second time
with his career at a peak, and as might have been expected,
there was a greater sense of permanence to what he was
doing when he returned. If the films in which he was to
appear during the following two decades would disappoint
the often vague and naïve expectations of his most critical admirers, at least those pictures were to include four
fine, unusual works as well as the less noteworthy productions in which the star nevertheless gave interesting
performances.

In the second category was *From The Terrace*, which,
though it came from 20th Century-Fox, might well have been
the sort of vehicle Warners would have chosen to repeat the
success of *The Young Philadelphians*. John O'Hara's novel
might have been a better literary source than Richard
Powell's, but even though Ernest Lehman wrote the screenplay, *From The Terrace* is decidedly less entertaining than the
previous film. Both are set in Philadelphia, and both chart the
rise to success and riches of an attractive opportunist. Both,

needless to say, have last-minute reformations of character in the opportunist.

Paul plays Alfred Eaton, who returns from World War I to find his mother (Myrna Loy) an alcoholic who is involved with a lover as well as the bottle, and his wealthy, sardonic father showing feeling only in mourning Alfred's long-dead older brother. It becomes Alfred's ambition to eclipse his father in affluence, and he leaves home and the family mill in order to join an engineering venture with a friend. He then meets the socialite and heiress Mary St John (Joanne), steals her from her psychiatrist-fiancé (Patrick O'Neal) and marries her only to neglect her for his business interests. These prosper when he saves from drowning the grandson of James Duncan MacHardie (Felix Aylmer), a Wall Street financier. Alfred joins his firm, while Mary rejoins her social set and is soon back in the arms of her former fiancé. On a business trip, Alfred encounters Natalie Benzinger (Ina Balin), an unspoiled girl with whom he is soon in love. But MacHardie's son-in-law Creighton Duffy (Howard Cline) hires detectives who photograph the lovers in bed, and with the evidence, Duffy hopes to blackmail Alfred into aiding him in a questionable deal. MacHardie has a puritanical aversion to promiscuity or even divorce in his staff, but at a meeting at which he will be offered a partnership, Alfred repudiates the rat-race, rejects married life with Mary and goes off to be reunited with Natalie.

There is no need to dwell on the merits and demerits of *From The Terrace* — a film that dwells on itself for an interminable 144 minutes. It is so boring that it comes as a distinct relief when the detectives break in a door to photograph Alfred and Natalie in bed — a moment if not of real drama then sufficiently noisy to arouse any audience from its torpor. Lehman dilutes the raw material of O'Hara's original, which has two wives and two mistresses and lets Alfred go to blazes in a big way, and the picture drifts glossily from one tableau of high life to another, gradually devoting more and more of its attention to a love-affair that would be banal even by the standards of romance in television commercials. Alfred's motivation is never clear, and Natalie, though she looks attractive, scarcely exists as a character, instead being one of Hollywood's most vacuous symbols of goodness and purity.

Paul and Joanne perform with professional aplomb. Carrying this dead weight on his back, Paul of course has the more difficult task, but though he sometimes looks understandably glum, his acting is good enough to generate some degree of identification. Joanne coruscates bitchily, probably enjoying herself, and she is almost too good when she makes her last sexual play for Alfred, who wearily rejects her. At that stage, she certainly seems more attractive than the wax doll who is waiting to be reunited with him on stepping-stones in the middle of a mountain-stream. (A commercial, surely. But dentifrice? Menthol cigarettes?) Not for the last time, Paul, in the boardroom-meeting, pulls a film into shape, charges it powerfully with the authority of his playing. In both good and bad productions, this ability to dominate and command at critical points was to become a familiar feature of his career.

Interviewed on the set during the picture's making, Joanne took a light-hearted view of her on-screen marriage break-up with Paul, denying that acting out such scenes made her in any way anxious or uneasy. 'On the contrary,' she said. 'It's a relief. We get all our hostilities worked off on the set. Then when we get home — wow!' But if Joanne was not superstitious about this marital calamity on celluloid, her mother was — 'when she heard about this she cried'. Naturally, the line the interviewer took was *faux-naïf*, especially as the Newmans, obvious love-birds, had been snapped by a photographer in a lonely corner of the set in the midst of an embrace that had nothing to do with the picture. However, if acting in *From The Terrace* provided almost a form of therapy — psychodrama before the term became current — it was also, in the end, taxing work. 'I'm exhausted,' Joanne admitted. 'We've been shooting seven days a week. That's to get the picture finished in time for Paul's *Exodus* exodus.'

Nobody could dispute *From The Terrace*'s great commercial success, but there were those by now who talked and wrote uneasily of Paul's choice of properties. Furthermore, though the film might have done its job in providing roles for both husband and wife in the same production, prophets of doom were not slow to point out that the record for husband-and-wife teams, both in terms of finding suitable vehicles and in terms of achievement, had been fairly lamentable. Such prophets were to be proved right *and* contradicted by later events, for though they could not at that time have imagined that Paul might direct Joanne to great effect, they were correct in their implied prediction of films starring both Paul and Joanne that would in general be poorly received.

In his invaluable book *A Biographical Dictionary Of The Cinema*, David Thomson writes that Paul's 'contempt for *Exodus* shows his poor understanding of the cinema'. If that statement is true, Paul Newman is in good company: there are undoubtedly many who love the cinema but are at the same time extremely uneasy about Otto Preminger's contribution to it. Nevertheless, for reasons that are never easy to comprehend, Preminger has become a vogue-figure, in whose work critics detect surprising profundities and a 'cool' that they categorize as objective authority rather than anonymity. There can be no doubt that Preminger is a controversial figure, but when, in 1960, Paul joined the cast of *Exodus*, his expectations were probably high. For all his dictatorial reputation, Preminger was fresh from a great commercial and critical success, *Anatomy Of A Murder*, a typical sprawling, diffuse and daring (in terms of defying censorship) picture that grossed $4 million in the United States and another million in the rest of the world. Furthermore, there could not have been one prominent leading-man who was not hungry for the role of Ari Ben Canaan, the leader of the Palestinian underground. Paul Newman, who was now synonymous with big box-office, secured the part.

He, Joanne and baby Elinor left for Israel, where, with his usual thoroughness, Paul spent several weeks to develop a feeling for the country and its people. He has sometimes been referred to as a non-Jewish actor playing a Haganah fighter, but the description is at best half-correct, and when one considers, on the other hand, that the star had a somewhat disturbing Jewish-Catholic background, it may be that a measure of rare personal identification ultimately illuminated his performance.

Preminger's headquarters in Haifa, where filming began, was the Hotel Zion, and shooting, which was scheduled to begin on 27th March 1960, was timetabled to last a mere fourteen weeks — a breathtaking prospect if account was taken of the scope of the story and the length of the final cut — three-and-a-half hours' running-time. The day after Paul arrived, he asked Preminger whether they might talk, a request to which the director readily acceded. Paul explained that he had studied the script, but when he produced several sheets covered with ideas and suggestions that he proceeded to read out, anybody who knew Preminger's view of the respective functions of actors and directors could have predicted his response.

When Paul had finished his recital, Preminger remarked mordantly, 'Very interesting suggestions. If you were directing the picture, you would use them. But I do not like them. As I am directing the picture, I shan't use them!'

Regardless of the rights and wrongs of that encounter, only a fool would have been surprised that there was a bad chemistry (Willi Frischauer, Preminger's biographer, uses the word 'antagonism') between the two men during the shooting of *Exodus*. Nevertheless, with a professional like Paul Newman, it is absurd to imply — as some have done — that there is a wooden quality to his acting in the film and that it is the result of his clash with the director. Nothing in the Newman personality justifies the idea of such pettiness, even as an involuntary reaction, and the star's standards are too high to allow personal considerations to affect his work in that way.

But the picture was not a happy experience for Paul, and whether because of that or because it received a mauling from the critics, or perhaps for both reasons, he cannot, according to remarks Joanne made during a television interview, bear either to talk or think about *Exodus*.

With too many strands to weave into its narrative fabric, the film undoubtedly sprawls and meanders, and as though it is five movies run consecutively, it sags badly at the end of sections. Nevertheless, it has some splendid set-pieces, even though it may be a dubious account of the birth of Israel in 1947. Many of the flaws are inherent in Dalton Trumbo's screenplay, which, though it organizes its mass of material adroitly enough, grinds out exposition rather obviously and falls back on rhetoric at the film's climaxes.

As Ari Ben Canaan, Paul makes a stern and preoccupied leader, and his style has a simplicity that is almost austere. In his entire career, only one other performance — as John Russell in *Hombre*, filmed six years later — rivals this one for economy. Yet the manner is authentic and carries authority, and the man's scepticism and refusal to trust even friends is typical of the star's screen-persona. In a difficult and superbly played role as an American widow drawn through love of Ari into the Jewish cause, it is left to the beautiful Eva Marie Saint to coax a modicum of tenderness from him, and his acting is for once devoid of the controversial Newman charm — unless it flickers in the comic-scene with Peter Lawford already described. Through his enviable power to project emotion thrillingly to audiences, it is Paul who singlehandedly brings *Exodus* to its climax. At the end of the picture, his oration over the twin graves of an Arab and a Jewess, both of them friends, transcends the limitations of writing that might have been more striking, and has a purity and passion in its impatient longing for peace that are truly moving. The least showy of his performances, this one is impressively characterized by understatement.

Such a quality was not what many reviewers had come to expect, and they voiced their disappointment at missing the star's more bravura aspects as well as their dissatisfaction with the movie's length, its simplification of complicated issues and its reluctance to offend anyone except the Nazis. Plodding worthiness found few plaudits among the critics, and there is a story that at a Hollywood preview the wit Mort Sahl stood up after three hours, addressed himself to Preminger and pleaded, 'Otto, let my people go'.

Despite reviews that described *Exodus* as a 'Jewish Western' and Preminger's 'Matso Opera', the movie was a worldwide success and grossed more than a million dollars for its direc-tor. In the Newman canon, it was Paul's second biggest grosser, exceeded in its takings only, thus far, by *Butch Cassidy And The Sundance Kid*. Even so, he and Preminger have never worked together again.

In 1966, the founding of the State of Israel was to receive a more worthy cinematic treatment in Melville Shavelson's *Cast A Giant Shadow*, which came much closer to doing justice to its theme. Ironically, while *Exodus* thrived at the box-office, *Cast A Giant Shadow* flopped. Shavelson, a jack-of-all-trades in the cinema, was associated with some of Bob Hope's better films, and he was to join with Joanne and Paul as producer, director and writer of *A New Kind Of Love*, the comedy that teamed husband and wife disastrously in 1963.

No matter what its star thought about it, *Exodus* was extremely popular as a Paul Newman film. He was paid his $200,000 for it, and at this stage, he had both fame and riches—enough for most men but not for an actor of his gifts. What he yet needed, what had thus far in his career persistently eluded him, was a real critical success in the cinema.

Once again, that almost incredible Newman luck came to his aid, and his very next picture, *The Hustler*, provided him with co-workers who included a great director (Robert Rossen), a great cameraman (Eugene Shuftan) and a great editor (Dede Allen). Not least important, it also offered him his first role of real stature — Eddie Felson. For whereas Rocky Graziano had a tangible, clear goal and both Anthony Judson Lawrence in *The Young Philadelphians* and Alfred Eaton in *From The Terrace* had great, if ignoble, ambitions, Eddie is in the grip of a divine obsession, haunted by the idea of being the best, an original, a great artist who will surpass even himself.

Fast Eddie is a pool-shark (hence the title) who tours the country, beating the suckers for money by masking his brilliance until the stakes are high enough for him to make a killing. When he comes to New York with his partner and manager Charlie Burns (Myron McCormick), he has one idea: to play and beat the champion of fifty states, Minnesota Fats (Jackie Gleason). But as victory looms, Eddie loses his nerve, drinks too much and sees the triumph, along with all his savings, pass to the cooler, more experienced man. Drained by the match, Eddie seeks comfort in the arms of Sarah Packard, a lame girl who is a heavy drinker with an undervalued literary talent that disturbs Eddie. It is Sarah who takes care of him when he hustles once too often and too hard in the wrong place, having his thumbs broken by toughs when they detect that he is a pool-shark. Sarah's feelings are much deeper than his, so that Eddie is reluctant to take her along on a trip to Louisville after Bert Gordon, a professional gambler, has agreed to manage him for a seventy-per-cent cut. Seeing Bert's sinister domination and manipulation of her lover, Sarah begins to drink even more heavily. At Louisville, Eddie takes on and beats a playboy-millionaire in a billiards-game, but Sarah, disillusioned by his behaviour and his new manager's perverted power, spends the night with Bert before committing suicide. Eddie splits with Bert and some time later returns to New York, where he brilliantly defeats Minnesota Fats. When Bert demands his cut, Eddie refuses to hand it over and denounces him as a destroyer. Bert allows him to leave but warns him that he will never again play in a big-time pool-hall.

   The Hustler derives from a fairly simple novel by Walter S. Tevis, but Robert Rossen and Sidney Carroll, as joint screen-writers, greatly add to and enrich the narrative texture. From the moment when Eddie admires the way Minnesota Fats performs — 'like he's playing a violin or something' — it is clear that the film is an allegory that takes in a large amount of territory — the nature of the artist, winning and losing, immaculateness of purpose, and the twisted pleasure of con- ·
niving at destruction. As with most allegories, the meaning can occasionally become blurred and dissatisfying, especially as no convincing correlative can be found for the money that Eddie seems eager enough to hang on to, even though the whole force of the drama implies that he plays Minnesota Fats a second time purely for the sake of winning, not for material benefit. Nevertheless, *The Hustler* is all but a great movie. It completely understands its background, if not every one of its characters, and it disdains smoothing out the lives it depicts or treating artistically such tired settings as a bus depot in the small hours or New York at dawn. Rossen films pool seriously, as though he expects us to find it intrinsically interesting, and this failure to patronize brings back memories of his *Body And Soul*, in which another girl fought for a man's soul — on that occasion a fighter played by an earlier powerful star, John Garfield.

In the later film, as Sarah, Piper Laurie has the most difficult — because imperfectly conceived — role among the principals. To those who had missed or overlooked her performance in *Until They Sail*, her acting must have come as a revelation, the more so if they had known her only from Universal's Westerns on sand, with Tony Curtis or Rock Hudson. There is a stillness about her playing that implies the depths not quite indicated by the script. When Eddie looks at the work-in-progress in her typewriter, he reads, 'We have a contract of depravity. All we have to do is pull a blind down.' As he puzzles over her words, her omniscient, sad eyes convey her knowledge that he resists the love that they can have, that he refuses the strongest comfort that they can offer each other as outcasts. She is the seer and prophet of the drama, and when Bert says all he wants is money, she smiles ironically, answering, 'Sure, just the money — and the aristocratic pleasure of seeing (men) fall apart. You're a Roman, Bert. You have to win them all.' In Louisville, she makes clear to Eddie, who is pleading with his manager to provide the money for his stake, that Bert can offer nothing but an embezzlement and perversion of Eddie's talent: 'Don't beg him. . . . Doesn't all this come through to you, Eddie? Doesn't any of this mean anything to you? That man, this place, the people — they wear masks, Eddie, and underneath the masks they're perverted, twisted, crippled. . . . Don't wear a mask, Eddie. You don't have to. . . . (Bert) hates you, because of what you are, because of what you have and he hasn't.'

It is a remarkable, haunting performance, full of the dark hues of the actress's voice, but it would exist in a vacuum without a complementary demonstration from the actor playing Bert Gordon. This *The Hustler* gets — in the shape of George C. Scott's masterly display. He embodies the spirit of denial to counterbalance Laurie's spirit of affirmation, but if he is the devil, he never overplays the part, his power being overlaid by an almost feline smoothness. There is an unassailable complacency to his pronouncement: 'Eddie, you're a born loser'; and when Sarah says, 'You own all the tomorrows because you buy them today, and you buy cheap' — he is superbly imperturbable as he retorts, 'Nobody has to sell.' But Scott never makes the mistake of having Bert

Gordon become totally inhuman — monstrous, yes, but with authentic humanity and weakness. It is there in his great cry to Eddie near the end: 'You owe me *money!*'; and he is shifty and cowardly about his part in Sarah's death in an exposed, despicable way that a lesser actor might have avoided.

But the picture is made, of course, for Paul Newman, and he is just as 'hot' in it as Fast Eddie is on one of his winning streaks. The acting is beautifully paced, with intelligent shifts of mood and emphasis. Those detractors who call Paul self-regarding provide an appropriate label for his early sequences, in which he *is* self-regarding — and that is the right quality for a character who is, at that stage, weak and overplays his charm. Elsewhere, Paul hits the right note of tender exasperation with his partner when Charlie talks only of money — 'You still don't see, do you, Charlie?'; and he is no less than brilliant when he states his artist's credo to Sarah in the sort of speech that looks, once you have seen the film, unusually eloquent on paper until you reflect that memory supplements with the inflexions and nuances of a superbly shaded interpretation: 'Anything can be great. I don't care — bricklaying can be great if a guy *knows* — if he knows what he's doing and why and can make it come off. When I'm going, when I'm really going, I feel like a — like a jockey must feel. He's sitting on this horse — he's got all that speed and power underneath him. He's coming into the straight, and the pressure's on, and he *knows* — just feels when to let it go and how much. 'Cos he's got everything working for him — timing, touch. . . . It's a great feeling, boy, it's a real great feeling when you're right and you know you're right. Like all of a sudden I got oil in my arm — the pool-cue's part of me. You know, the pool-cue's got nerves in it. It's a piece of wood, but it's got nerves in it. I feel the roll of those balls — don't have to look. You just know. You make shots that nobody's ever made before. You play that game the way nobody's ever played it before.'

The excitement and passion that Paul injects into these words move audiences as much as they do Sarah, who replies, 'Some men never get to feel that way about anything.' But if, like this one, Paul's solos are often brilliant, it is untrue that he is not a good ensemble player. If he had not been so revealed previously, *The Hustler* reveals him as a good listener, sensitive and generous enough to 'feed' Laurie and Scott self-effacingly when he knows the focus of interest is on them. Thus, given a marvellous last speech that has resonances of the funeral oration in *Exodus*, he emerges, as Eddie Felson should, full of power — reborn and strengthened where he was formerly weak. Paul's lack of any reluctance to display vulnerability and self-indulgence, his willingness (rare in a star) to subdue his talents to those of others, make the contrast all the more spectacular. As there so often is in the climaxes of Paul Newman's movies, there is that characteristic sense that he is summing up the dramatic argument, imperiously distilling the essence of the picture's themes. The words are important: when he has so often been so lucky with his writers, it would be unfair and foolish to deny that. But it would be equally inappropriate to minimize the emotional force and conviction with which he endows lines like these: 'How can I lose? . . . It's not enough that you just have talent, you gotta have character, too. Yeah, an' I sure got character now. Picked it up in a hotel-room in Louisville. . . . We really stuck the knife in her, didn't we, Bert? . . . Oh, we really gave it to her good. . . . Then we twisted it, didn't we, Bert? Course, maybe that doesn't stick in your throat, 'cos you spit it out the way you spit out everything else. But it sticks in mine. I loved her, Bert. I traded her in on a pool-game. But that wouldn't mean anything to you, because who did you ever care about? Just win — win, you said — that's the important thing. You don't know what winning is, Bert. You're a loser! 'Cos you're dead inside and you can't live unless you make everything else dead around you. Too high, Bert. The price is too high. If I take it, she never lived, she never died. And we both know that's not true, Bert, don't we? She lived, she died.'

At a more prosaic and purely technical level, Paul looks astonishingly good in the important and lengthy pool-sequences. In close-ups of the cue-work, Willie Mosconi's hands are seen, and clever cutting enhances the illusion that Paul and Jackie Gleason are actually making their shots. Both actors, however, were coached so that their movements at least had a surface authenticity.

The Hustler eventually took nine Academy Award nominations, including Newman's for Best Actor. In the end, only Eugene Shuftan, for his cinematography, actually won an award, but as a sort of consolation-prize, Paul was to win the British Academy Award.

For Rossen's picture, it is worth remarking, the company had three weeks of rehearsals, using the technique perfected in television in which the floor of the rehearsal-hall is taped to indicate the limits and dimensions of the actual sets that will be used in filming. A great believer in such rehearsal periods, Paul is prepared to devote his time to them without salary.

If *The Hustler* confirmed or reconfirmed Paul Newman's stardom with public and critics alike, it also reinforced the *nature* of that stardom. Over the years, this had been defining itself steadily—a matter more of accident than of voluntary, controlled policy. From the beginning, there had been Paul's aversion, if not outright hostility, to the press, his cherishing of privacy or even anonymity. To this predilection had been added a series of accidents (more or less)—roles in which he had played loners and misfits (*The Rack, Until They Sail, The Long Hot Summer*), men driven by ambition (*The Young Philadelphians, From The Terrace*), heroes perfecting a craft or fulfilling a special destiny (*Somebody Up There Likes Me, The Left-Handed Gun, Exodus*) and, most recently, an artist caught up in a metaphysical struggle (*The Hustler*). Whether he had intended to or not, Paul had established both by his life-style and the parts he played the persona of the traditional star—remote, larger-than-life, superhuman (if not super-virile), singled out for a special fate or special suffering. It was an image that had served well enough stars as different as Ronald Colman, Greta Garbo and Paul Muni. And there was something interestingly old-fashioned about it.

On the stage, Laurence Olivier had helped make himself an idol through what might have been termed the 'Great Man Syndrome'—an addiction to roles of inherent stature, such as the Prince of Denmark, Henry V, Richard III, Oedipus Rex, Titus Andronicus and Thomas à Becket. More recently and in the cinema, Charlton Heston had manifested parallel preferences, playing such great names in history as Andrew Jackson, the Cid, John the Baptist, General Gordon and Mark Antony. Less obviously and certainly less deliberately, Paul had by 1961 made himself equally distant and elevated—a star whom it was easy to admire and with whom it was natural to sympathize; but not one who ever really seemed like the common man or the boy next door. It was to be left to such stars as Michael Caine and Dustin Hoffman, following the example set by the earlier William Holden, to reduce to vanishing point the gap between stars and public. With his jealously guarded private life, recalling Colman, and his roles that defied simple identification, not unlike those of Garbo, Paul Newman was arguably one of the last stars. As a person, he retained an aura of mystery and withdrawal. As a screen-symbol, he was almost always an outsider or one who would end up as an outcast or martyr—an alienated modern hero. What *The Hustler* had almost ideally refined, the rest of his career would repeat and consolidate. The inaccessibility of both man and star would continue to be a potent ingredient in the Newman chemistry.

6

Marking Time

The couple who had three years before collapsed into each other's arms with relief at finally being pronounced man and wife were discovering that marriage, however nourishing, had its inevitable stresses, but also that there were two sides to every difficulty — and that the negative side, with each passing year, bound them together just as surely as anything else.

Their differences in personality, for example.

A decade later, Paul was to comment, 'For two people with almost nothing in common, we have an uncommonly good marriage.' Just as the Newmans' marriage was never to sound like a public-relations exercise, there was no denying the implied contrasts. Paul enjoyed drinking beer — according to various estimates, twenty or thirty cans a day, and in the era before ring-pull cans came on the market, part of his almost invariably casual dress was (besides jeans and T-shirt) a beer-can opener worn on a chain around his neck. His interest in motor-racing had yet to move into the high gear that it would find in the mid seventies, but he enjoyed shooting pool and un-equivocally masculine pursuits. Unlike his wife, who was a fairly original thinker, he had ideas that tended towards the conventional, his attitudes sometimes seeming Victorian to Joanne, who nevertheless respected them.

She, on the other hand, was mainly interested in literature, art and the ballet. Though Paul, on sufferance, would later attend ballet performances, he drew the line in no uncertain manner at active participation. (A point-blank refusal that scarcely makes him unique among males, American or of other nationalities.) Those whom Joanne liked and admired included Segovia, Nureyev, Franco Corelli, Gore Vidal and Albert Finney. Attempting a complementary list, Paul came up with Jean Simmons and Rosie Fontayne ('A cook we knew,' Joanne explained). While Paul often seemed painfully inarticulate, Joanne was becoming famous for her eloquent interviews. He drank beer, and her favourite tipple was sherry.

True, they were both filmstars. But as actors they were of dissimilar temperaments—Joanne brilliant and intuitive, intensely ambitious in the best, most artistic sense; Paul 'cerebral', painstaking, ever doubtful about both his own ability and the nature of the profession, enjoying preparation and research far more than performance. And it was just beginning to become obvious to the perceptive—including the Newmans themselves—that Paul, whether he liked it or not, would continue to be a star, whereas Joanne's aesthetic destiny lay in what might have been more correctly described as character-acting. Partly because of his looks, Paul had the larger-than-life, unique and unmistakable persona that went with stardom, but Joanne had already shown her ability to subdue herself entirely to a role, to change her looks, deportment and speech according to the demands of her work. Of the two, she was the virtuoso-performer, with the chameleonic qualities that distinguish a José Ferrer or a Julie Harris. Significantly, she has rarely looked as beautiful on screen as she does in real life.

But the differences between husband and wife were more stimulating than divisive. In the most literal sense, they might not have been sharing their interests and hobbies, but each was curious about and sympathetic towards the pastimes of the other. They discovered that their politics were virtually identical. Moving with caution, they had spent seven years getting to know each other before matrimony; theirs had been no plunge into wedded bliss. As their shared happiness evolved, there were naturally those occasions when their plans conflicted, their likes and aversions clashed. They adjusted to such difficulties through what Joanne has described as 'sensible compromise'. If they really *were* complete opposites (a phrase she has also used), so what? They loved each other, were absorbed—but not preoccupied—with each other; and 'Think,' Joanne has often suggested to journalists, 'how boring a marriage it would be if we were the same.'

Paul the man might or might not have been something of a square. He seemed so (not to say chauvinistic) in an unfortunate interview in which he appeared to describe Joanne as 'steak he could have at home'—a remark that Women's Libbers did not allow him to forget. Nevertheless, he had married a New

Woman. (A misnomer if ever there was one. Though New Women did not appear in large numbers until the sixties and seventies, at which time they became vocal and organized, they have existed for centuries.) Joanne had no intention of becoming a mere adjunct to her more famous spouse. She was beginning to bristle at being asked again and again, 'Aren't you Mrs Paul Newman?' or, even worse, 'Who are you?' The very worst, however, was reserved for years later, and Joanne finally exploded one day when a girl stopped her on the street with the inquiry: 'Aren't you Scott Newman's mother?'

When Joanne began her career, she had fierce, defined professional and personal ambitions. For the first, she wanted to play a role to perfection, and some would have said that she had already done that by the time *The Three Faces Of Eve* was completed. As for personal ambitions, one of the greatest was to have four babies whom she would bring up as normal, healthy children.

But as in all other lives, there were developments and obstacles that she could not have foreseen. One was her changing attitude to parenthood, about which more will be heard later; and in fact she was to have only three children. Then her plans had scarcely taken into account the possibility of joining her life to that of an international sex-symbol. Nobody minimizes talents or personal qualities by marrying them, but Joanne has repeatedly pointed out that Paul snores in his sleep, that he is the father of six children and that no woman continually thinks of her husband as a sex-symbol.

Then there is the professional partnership of the Newmans. It was to be another fifteen years before they would admit publicly that it had never really worked, but even though they were to persist with co-starring ventures, there was already, as early as *Paris Blues*, released in 1961, more than a suspicion that success as a team would elude them as it had done other husband-and-wife acting-combinations. Furthermore, Joanne, determined to be an equal partner in marriage, had to become resigned to a professional disparity: any picture in which she and Paul appeared together was to be known automatically as 'a Paul Newman picture' — never 'a Joanne Woodward picture'.

On Paul's side, matters might have looked different. It was

Joanne's Academy Award that adorned the mantelpiece, and the prize was to go on eluding him.

These were some of the obvious and the subtle stresses at work in one of the most durable of the famous marriages of our time. But they were outweighed by a sense of fulfilment and achievement as the new decade advanced.

1961 was the year of Paul's triumph in *The Hustler*, and that September, Joanne was to give birth to a second daughter, Melissa.

With high hopes, husband and wife starred together for the fourth time in their second picture for Martin Ritt, *Paris Blues*. Confident in Ritt's directorial ability, Paul believed that the property's treatment of such topics as race, narcotics, jazz and expatriate Americans discovering Europe would ensure success. Primarily, though, the picture was yet another example of the old-fashioned 'concerto-movie' such as Charles Vidor's *Rhapsody*; and the track-record for films about music and musicians — with such exceptions as Irving Rapper's stylish and artificial *Deception* or the two-thirds excellent *Humoresque*, directed by Jean Negulesco — had never been all that good, either commercially or critically.

Paris Blues was not to join the exceptions, being one of those films that are pleasant enough to watch for the first time but too bland to leave an enduring impression. The plot concerns an American trombonist, Ram Bowen (Paul), and his black friend Eddie Cook (Sidney Poitier) whose band is a big attraction at a Left Bank *cave* in Paris, with the owner of which, Marie Seoul (Barbara Laage), Ram has an amorous but undemanding relationship. When the famous trumpeter Wild Man Moore (Louis Armstrong) arrives in Paris, Ram makes up his mind to take to him a concerto he has written. Coincidentally, Ram meets Lillian Corning (Joanne) and her black companion Connie Lampson (Diahann Carroll), two American tourists. Wild Man promises to show the concerto to an impresario, and when the girls visit the club, Ram, drawn to Connie, nevertheless has his interest diverted by Lillian. Connie and Eddie likewise fall in love, but neither affair is without friction. Connie wants Eddie to return to the States, where he could help win racial equality. When the impresario rejects his concerto, Ram is prepared to return with Lillian when she goes home, but at the last moment, to her despair, he backs out. Though Ram puts his ambition ahead of his personal life, the more casual Eddie promises to join Connie.

The film was shot on location with French technicians and has at least a surface-authenticity. Ultimately, though, the impression is of imitation *nouvelle vague*, the matt finish being dull and trying. Four hands were involved in the screen-play, which was derived from a rather weak novel, and it is diffuse, feebly motivated and unoriginal, with excursions into drug-addiction that are totally irrelevant. Nevertheless, Ritt's handling of sexual relationships is extraordinarily sensitive, and the sympathetic playing of Paul and Joanne is fascinating to watch as their affair passes from faint animosity to reassessment and through tentative advances to an efflorescence of affection. Then, too, the alliance between Ram and his employer is so beautifully acted and directed that it seems almost more valid than the Ram-Lillian romance, thus creating an uneasy imbalance. If the relationship between Eddie and Connie is less successfully established, it is partly because of feeble writing and partly because it lacks growth — the two lovers wander tirelessly around Paris and talk race-problems exhaustively and exhaustingly.

If, as seems likely, some of the film's dialogue was improvised, the results do nothing to commend the practice — essential as it may be to jazz, on the other hand, which *Paris Blues*, despite music by Duke Ellington and the presence and playing of Louis Armstrong, serves rather shabbily. Paul, however convincing as a lover, lacks credibility as a musician. Nevertheless, there is much to appreciate in *Paris Blues*, the four young people and the older, sadder mistress leaving pleasant but evanescent impressions.

The film's comparative failure must have been the harder for Paul to take coming so soon after *The Hustler*. Of course, the earlier picture's success had been on a highly gratifying scale, but after his acting as Eddie Felson had secured him a nomination, it was doubtless more than disappointing to see the Academy Award go to Maximilian von Schell for a sound but one-key performance in the stolid, empty *Judgment At Nuremberg*.

Nor was Paul's next picture, *Sweet Bird Of Youth*, to give him the opportunity he might have expected after having played Chance Wayne on the stage to rave-reviews, and his performance on the screen did not even win a nomination for the 1962 Academy Award.

But, then, as written and directed by Richard Brooks, *Sweet Bird Of Youth* is hardly the Tennessee Williams work that had been seen on Broadway four years earlier. (In Hollywood's sanitizing process, as Williams himself has pointed out, damage is usually done to the plays in the last couple of minutes; but, then, the author, too, often does a fair amount of harm at this stage — artistically.) Not entirely to appease censorship, the story is streamlined, simplified and given a happy ending. Syphilis and hysterectomy are abandoned in favour of the less daunting abortion; Chance *does* manage to see Heavenly Finley; and Tom Finley and his cronies merely disfigure Chance — and not too badly at that. Most significantly of all, however, the last shot shows Chance and Heavenly leaving town for what is presumably a happy future (compare page 84).

Milton Krasner's photography aids and abets by beautifying what should have been sordid and repulsive. On the credit side, though, the acting is generally excellent, especially that of Geraldine Page, who, if she seems too young for her role, gives a fine performance in which humour is the unexpected ingredient. Her witty, polished playing would not be out of place in a comedy of manners (which *Sweet Bird Of Youth*, unintentionally, perhaps becomes), and she ditches Chance with superb, bitchy style.

Paul likewise appears too young for his part. His Chance looks too intact and lacks the desperation that might have made the role more credible. Betrayed by the script, he fails to convey the true impression of a male whore. But he cannot be blamed, especially as, within the limitations of this aborted context, he performs admirably.

Even so, the sense of waste was alarming. It could all have been so different, most of all for the star. If only the play had not been tampered with and if only Elia Kazan had directed the film as he had previously directed the play. Actors are prodigal and eloquent in their praise of Kazan. Andy Griffith has said that he knows people and how to make actors feel important. Lee Remick has described working with him as a revelation during which the director draws out the best from his players. Kim Hunter found that he gave her confidence and understanding, while Ben Gazzara was inspired by Kazan's tuition at the Actors' Studio. Eileen Heckart once said that he had four ideas for every one that she had.

Speaking of the Broadway production of *Sweet Bird Of Youth*, Paul Newman put it simply: 'For the most part, I relied on the director, Elia Kazan, for what I did. He has broad shoulders. His invention, imagination and patience are extraordinary.' These qualities helped shape a fascinating and remarkable Chance Wayne on the stage. Furthermore, the *continuity* of stage-acting, combined with Kazan's guidance in rehearsals, aided Paul in evolving the characterization. As he once said: 'When I begin working on a part, I find that the first things I do are usually wrong. After rehearsals start, however, I find that I get rid of the wrong things bit by bit, until I get the part so that it feels fairly comfortable and fairly right.' Even so, he asserted that there were areas of Chance Wayne that still eluded him after ten months on Broadway—the self-criticism, one might assume, of a perfectionist.

Paul's assessment of his own acting could have been accurate, but it was good enough nonetheless to thrill audiences and move them deeply. *That* Chance Wayne was fated never to be seen on the screen.

After *Sweet Bird Of Youth*, Paul found for himself the sort of change of pace much loved by actors and almost equally mistrusted by the fans of stars. Reprising his 1955 television-performance as The Battler, he played a so-called cameo-role in Martin Ritt's *Adventures Of A Young Man* (also known as *Hemingway's Adventures Of A Young Man*)—a film that is a good (or bad) example of the limitations that may be imposed on a gifted director by an inferior script. This one, written by A. E. Hotchner, is based on the Nick Adams stories, but it does little to convey the ethos of Hemingway or to suggest the personality of a young man genuinely interested in writing. In any case, there is something offensively naïve about the notion, watered down in Hotchner but undiluted in Hemingway, that a writer may roam around 'collecting' experience as a tourist gathers souvenirs—an idea belonging more to journalism than to literature. Ritt's film might be contrasted with an earlier film from the same studio (Fox), *The Snows Of Kilimanjaro*, joint masterpiece of screen-writer Casey Robinson and director Henry King, which maintains its quality despite a tacked-on but irrelevant happy ending. Starting from a Hemingway short story, Robinson expands the piece in a way that presents the quintessence of Hemingway with perhaps something a good deal better, too, belonging to Robinson alone. In *Kilimanjaro*, Harry Street (Gregory Peck) has both the ambition and the passion of a writer; he is damaged, he grows, he bitterly learns to know himself as man and author. In *Adventures Of A Young Man*, Nick (a gauche Richard Beymer) clearly does nothing of the sort. No matter what happens, he is unchanged, he learns nothing, and when he goes off at the end of the picture to write about what he has seen, we can be thankful that at least we don't have to read the resulting book.

All this having been said, Ritt's fluent direction, it must be added, does more than might have been expected with the unpromising material. The best sequences are those around the Michigan lakes, with the wind blowing—a visual metaphor of Nick's restlessness that is effortlessly captured by Lee Garmes' superb cinematography. The cast struggles manfully with flat, diffuse dialogue, and those who emerge best include Paul and those two great actors Juano Hernandez and Arthur Kennedy. There is a lovely score by Franz Waxman.

For Paul, there were two dangers in playing his role. First, there was a measure of daring in his accepting so small a part. One school of thought insists that stardom is a matter of big parts in big pictures, and that any deviation from that principle puzzles the fans and imperils the star's stature. Then there was the fact that Paul was almost unrecognizable. His features thickened, his mouth open in repose and his voice a hoarse croak, he practised the sort of acting, essentially aided by make-up, that few stars have ever risked in their prime. (Lon Chaney did it almost entirely as a series of feats with make-up; Paul Muni, more interestingly, sought always to escape from his own character into another, changing his appearance as an adjunct to the process.) With actors like

Paul Newman, physical disguise can lead to a strange, even disconcerting, muffling of star-allure. John Huston's rather silly *The List Of Adrian Messenger*, made the following year, was to show — with its clutch of heavily masquerading stars and an invitation to audiences to guess their identity — that such players as Burt Lancaster, Frank Sinatra, Robert Mitchum and Tony Curtis lose much of their magic when they are deprived of familiar physical aspects and the equally familiar resonances of their usual voices.

Still, for an actor who aspired to virtuoso display, *Adventures Of A Young Man* was an interesting excursion — even if in an unworthy picture.

It was, however, no *more* than an interesting excursion. *Sweet Bird Of Youth* had been abortive, and *Paris Blues* had been a cruel disappointment, not only to admirers of Paul Newman but also, perhaps, to all concerned. Only slightly marred by its clouded allegory, *The Hustler* had been a genuine peak, but *The Hustler* was two years ago. Would Paul never again get back to the same level? Those with his best interests at heart must have asked themselves the question with some anxiety.

And then came *Hud*.

7

Hero or Villain?

Released in 1963, two years after his previous success with
The Hustler, Martin Ritt's *Hud* once more gave Paul an
enormous critical and commercial success, though, as we
shall see, there was one clear dissenting voice about the
casting of its star. Like *The Hustler*, *Hud* contains a com-
pelling characterization of the loner who recurs in so many
Newman pictures, and Paul's acting, though immensely
authoritative and encompassing a wide range, nevertheless
projects the coldness, often overlooked, that lies somewhere
near the heart of his best work.

Hud is an adaptation that develops and enriches Larry
McMurtry's novel, *Horseman, Pass By*. Seventeen-year-old
Lon Bannon (Brandon de Wilde) is the faintly puzzled bystander in the struggle between his grandfather Homer (Melvyn Douglas) and Homer's hell-raising son Hud, Lon's uncle
(Paul). Impatient to take control of Homer's Texas ranch,
Hud initiates proceedings to have the old man declared
legally incompetent. But when his complete herd, stricken
by hoof-and-mouth disease, has to be destroyed, Homer
is heartbroken and dies after a fall from his horse. ('It don't
take long to kill things,' he laments, 'not like it does to
grow 'em.') Lon rejects the existence that Hud offers to
share with him on the ranch, which is rich with oil, and
he departs to lead his own life.

Polemical drama would be an unfortunate label with which
to stick *Hud*, partly because the term sounds stuffy, but mainly
because it is the characters, so memorably full of life, who
command total absorption — not any philosophy implied by
their mode of existence. Hud himself, for example, is so well
written and acted that moral stickers such as 'good' and 'bad'
seem absurd and irrelevant, even if the evasion of such labels
is, in Pauline Kael's eyes, typical of the film makers.

All this is not to deny the ideological clash in the screenplay by Irving Ravetch and Harriet Frank Jr. Hud and

Homer are revealed as man of fact and man of idea, the one doomed to be destroyed by the other. (If Homer had not obligingly died, it seems pretty certain that Hud would have had his way and got the old man certified.) Hud makes his view of the world unmistakably clear: 'You take the sinners away from the saints, and you're lucky to be left with Abraham Lincoln. So I say let us dip our bread into some of that gravy while it is still hot. . . . I always say the law is meant to be interpreted in a lenient manner. And that's what I try to do. Sometimes I lean to one side of it and sometimes to the other.' To which Homer, sternly a man of principle, replies, 'You don't care about people, Hud. You don't give a damn about them . . . You just live for yourself, and that makes you not fit to live with.'

But the screenwriters are too intelligent to see this juxtaposition of two powerful men as a simple one. To the end, Hud and Homer retain a sympathy and respect for each other — spirits of affirmation and denial, impossible to divorce. As Hud says to Lon, 'You don't know the whole story. Him and me fought many a round together. But I guess you could say I helped him as much as he helped me.'

Hud is rightly named, for there can be no doubt about who is the central character. Hud Bannon is the adamant against which others wreck or prove themselves, and Paul Newman satisfies the demands of direction and writing by creating a totality rather than a facet: the performance is solid and deep. His remarkable features have seldom reflected so much. Power by this time came easily to him, and he injects his unique force into his attack on Homer's self-righteousness — 'You been handing out the ten tablets of law from whatever hill you could find to climb on ever since I was a kid.' But as Homer tells us, 'Even Hud can get lonesome once in a while', and Paul manages to combine the antitheses of the character, his complicated mixture of hedonism and misanthropy, sensitivity and ruthlessness, sardonic humour (by now, also a Newman speciality) and grave respect. When Hud is told that he is rough on everybody, there is just a trace of compassion to Paul's murmured, 'So they tell me'. The star never allows his concept to become sentimentalized, balancing such moments with the bravado of his summing-up of the complete realist's philosophy: 'This world is so full of crap a man's going to get into it sooner or later whether he's careful or not.' Again, the performance has room for Hud's tenderness in his attitude to Lon, something more than the mere words Paul utters. His mouth and eyes bespeak a sad wisdom as he advises the boy, 'Get all the good you can out of seventeen 'cause it sure wears out in one hell of a hurry'; and this same, almost tragic, sense of ephemerality is present in the gentle tones Paul uses when Hud, his remark lightly orchestrated by nocturnal cicadas, talks to Lon of the boy's dead father: 'I wonder if your daddy's hearing that grass now growing up over his grave.'

Paul has not always been fortunate in his directors, but there is never any doubt in this picture that actor's vision and director's are one and the same. Both are alive to the paradoxes of the man, and there is an impressively unresolved, satisfyingly ambiguous quality to the last view Ritt allows us of Hud — glimpsed behind the gauze of the screen-door, master of the house, strong, alone, shut in, shut out, lusting for life, solaced by the bottle, arrogant to the end.

Pointing persuasively to what she saw as the cynical or at least knowing manipulation of several themes, Pauline Kael found the dice loaded in terms of audience-response: Hud was overburdened with charm while Homer was a sanctimonious, desiccated bore. Martin Ritt, on the other hand, said that he considered Hud 'a bastard'. However, it is possible to regard both views as essentially oversimplified conceptions of the screenplay. Though Homer is not intended to be a bore (and, in Melvyn Douglas's splendid portrayal, there is nothing boring about his nostalgia, his moral sense and his contempt for the present), Hud *is* meant to be a charmer and is indeed so described by his own highly critical father. Homer speaks eloquently, on the other hand, about the look of the country changing because of 'the men we admire'. He is talking to Lon, and there can be no doubt that he has Hud in mind. Like Lon, we, the audience, should first be attracted and then repelled. Or should we? (Herein lies the art, if complications have anything to do with art.) The amiable rotter defies easy judgements.

Even so, we are still stuck with the problem of Paul Newman's charm. It may not be his fault, but his personal appeal
is so great that there is a real danger of his totally obscuring
the opportunism, arrogance, cynicism and contempt in the
character he plays. Ultimately, however, those who make
a film like *Hud* are asking of their audience considerably
more than an unthinking acceptance of bad guys and good
guys—even if, as Pauline Kael suggests, the moviemakers
blur the stereotypes the better to deceive us.

As usual, her arguments are not easy to refute, and she
writes of *Hud*'s star in terms of an insurance-policy taken
out by Ritt, Ravetch and Frank—their 'solid saleable property of Meissen and Biedermeier, in Paul Newman unfairly balanced against an innocent, unlikely Lon and a
Homer who evokes Polonius in *Hamlet*. In these words, she
takes the moviemakers to task: 'They could cast (Newman)
as a mean man and know that the audience would never
believe in his meanness. For there are certain actors who
have such extraordinary audience rapport that the audience
does not believe in their villainy except to relish it, as with
Brando; and there are others, like Newman, who in addition
to this rapport, project such a traditional heroic frankness
and sweetness that an audience dotes on them, seeks to protect them from harm and pain. Casting Newman as a mean
materialist is like writing a manifesto against the banking
system while juggling your investments so you can break
the bank.'

The language is eloquent and seductive, but whatever
the motives of the film-makers (and Miss Kael, of course,
is not naïve enough to believe that they *didn't* want to make
money), the logic of the argument is suspect. Audiences
relish the villainy of Hud, all right, even though they know
he is a heel. But that is not enough for Miss Kael. In an
argument whose full text extends over many pages, she attempts to turn Lon into a cipher ('that seventeen-year-old
blank sheet of paper') and Homer into a moralizing bore —
with neither of which views this writer can agree. Thus the
bad Hud is irresistibly attractive while the good Homer and
Lon are insipid and monotonous.

Rejecting this oversimplification, the film, one might

counter-argue, instead presents us with a moralist, in Homer, who is appealing *as well* and a Hud who is *both* a heel and a charmer. Surely *Hud* is the richer and stronger for such admixtures. Would the picture be more effective if Hud were totally repellent? And why, in those circumstances, should Lon either admire his uncle or be confused by the moral struggle between Hud and Homer? By the time the movie comes to a close, even Paul Newman's considerable charm and sexual allure cannot mask (except for the wilfully myopic) the callousness of Hud's attempt to get Homer certified, his sexual opportunism and the ultimately deadening nature of his materialism.

If it does nothing else, the debate at least demonstrates the many-layered fullness of *Hud*, and in any discussion of the film's merits and demerits, one important point should not be overlooked. If Hud really *is* the hero whom Pauline Kael sees presented for public approval, the American hero has at last become capable of rape. After a night on the town, Hud attempts to take by force the housekeeper Alma (Patricia Neal) and is prevented by Lon. (Alma was black in the original novel, in which her name was Halmea, and so the change of race was a predictable compromise — a point strangely missed by Pauline Kael in her otherwise relentless dissection of *Hud*'s concessions to the box-office.) To present a star attempting such an act was a form of pioneering — paving the way for the later antisocial deeds of figures like Clint Eastwood, James Coburn and Charles Bronson.

No matter how great the controversy about his casting, however, *Hud* is considerably more than a personal triumph for Paul Newman. Much of the credit for the movie's success must go to Martin Ritt, whose skill and control are patent from first to last — in his interpretation of an outstanding screenplay, in his handling of a great team of actors, in his sense of locations and in his brilliant direction of the sequence in which Homer's cattle are destroyed, an episode that is edited in masterly fashion, camera-angles selected so carefully that no steer is seen to die — and yet the whole so staged that one is left with an indelible impression of the slaughter's horrific efficiency. The late James Wong Howe captures with unfailing precision what Ritt selects — the dusty roads, the stark funeral chapel, the isolated ranch-house and the glittering chrome and glass of the town. Wong Howe was a cameraman whose greatness never seemed inhibited by dimensions as large as those of the Panavision screen.

Among other fine actors, Brandon de Wilde (to be prematurely and tragically killed a few years later in an automobile accident) is a happy choice for Lon, possibly at his best towards the close of the picture when he is offered conventional comfort on Homer's death—'He's gone to a better place.' With the unstressed simplicity of one who has learned a profound and enduring lesson (from Hud?), the boy replies, 'I don't think so. Not unless dirt is a better place than air.' Capable of the same clear yet unemphatic inflections, Patricia Neal invests Alma with a sympathetic combination of cynicism and dignity; her worldly tolerance and comprehension are a stimulating complement to Hud's misanthropy.

Never a director to trust music overmuch, Ritt limits Elmer Bernstein to sparse scoring in the form of a guitar solo that underlines the loneliness of the setting. Nevertheless, though one might wish there were more of it, the score works perfectly.

Hud was to take its share of the 1963 Academy Awards. Patricia Neal picked up the award for Best Actress, and Melvyn Douglas was honoured as Best Supporting Actor. An award went to James Wong Howe for Best Black and White Cinematography. However, though Paul obtained his third Academy Award nomination, the prize actually went to his co-star in *Paris Blues*, Sidney Poitier, for his performance in *Lilies Of The Field*.

Not for the first or last time, the selection seemed inscrutable. Poitier was good in his role, but it lacked the complexity of Hud Bannon and did not remotely approximate the same histrionic range. There were echoes of Ben Quick, the hero of *The Long Hot Summer*, in Hud, and Martin Ritt was later to say, 'We understood exactly what was original about Paul Newman and we wrote for that in *The Long Hot Summer*, *Hud* and *Hombre*.' Nevertheless, *Hud* is far removed from the conventional star-vehicle, and only an actor of considerable resources could have tackled the part to comparable effect. The dynamic range of Paul's performance far exceeded what Poitier had been able to accomplish in the slight but amiable *Lilies Of The Field*.

There were those who said that Newman, having been passed over once too often, was a marked man. He had bucked the system by clashing with Jack Warner. He was a loner and defier of convention. By preferring the East Coast to Hollywood, he had unforgivably insulted the movie-colony. And so on.

The truth was probably much more prosaic. Coveted in the industry, the Academy Awards have enjoyed a more dubious status outside it — perhaps because the annual selections have too frequently been imponderable and capricious. All too frequently, the prize has been awarded to obvious and showy performances, such as that given by Susan Hayward in *I Want To Live*. (Five times nominated, Hayward, a fine actress, gave numerous superior exhibitions in better films.) After fifty years in movies, the magnificently talented Edward G. Robinson was accorded an award a few months after his death — posthumous recognition that in no way atoned for the years of oversight. Once he was pushing seventy, John Wayne received what might have been termed a 'geriatric award' for quite conventional playing in *True Grit*. Sympathy and affection can, however, work for a star earlier in his career, and thus Elizabeth Taylor, having twice been passed over for *Raintree County* and *Cat On A Hot Tin Roof*, in neither of which she was exactly brilliant, won the accolade not long after her bereavement (the late Mike Todd) with a conventional showing in the lamentable *Butterfield 8*. The Oscar has also been handed to those who have ditched, however temporarily, their stereotypes, and thus James Cagney, jettisoning his tough-guy persona for a stint as song-and-dance man, found himself a winner for his acting in *Yankee Doodle Dandy*. Furthermore, not only these vagaries and eccentricities in selection have helped to bring the Academy Awards into question, if not disrepute, but also the widespread practice of launching expensive publicity campaigns to ensure the selectors' attention — both by stars and by such 'technical' experts as composers, cameramen and directors.

Being passed over yet again — and for a great performance — probably irked Paul, but though he might have
longed to be honoured by his peers, he must have experienced
the most profound satisfaction over his work in *Hud* — private
and personal gratification that more than compensated for the
public neglect.

That neglect was to continue, and years later, Joanne
was to attack the myopia of the Academy Awards selection
committee in these terms; '(Paul's) backing of liberal organi-
zations doesn't quite fit in with certain establishments.'

The year 1963 was significant for Paul's political activities,
which upset many other people besides the Hollywood
establishment. This was the year in which his commitment
was clearly to be seen by a large public for the first time.
He took part in the civil rights March on Washington and
participated in a fair-housing sit-in in Sacramento. He also
went to Gadsden, Alabama, for a rally on racial problems
led by Dr Martin Luther King. With him were Tony Franciosa, Marlon Brando and Virgil Frye, and all of them were
to be denied a meeting with the Mayor, who will possibly
be remembered for nothing else so much as dubbing this
illustrious thespian quartet 'rabble-rousers'. (That Paul
should join forces with Brando showed that, for all the irritation of those early notices comparing him with the other
star, he harboured no personal resentment towards the man.)
These events were to be the first overt or spectacular illustra-
tion of political affiliations that had previously manifested
themselves less obviously — Paul's stardom being only tentative — in the mid fifties with the Stevenson and Kennedy campaigns and were to continue through the sixties with public
statements against the US's commitment in Vietnam.

Just as unequivocally as any espousal of liberal causes,
a pattern of the Newmans' domesticity also defined itself
in the early sixties. To Joanne, California was 'a beautiful
woman dying of cancer', and she finally persuaded Paul,
never exactly a stalwart of the Hollywood colony, that they
should give up their Beverly Hills house and make their
permanent base in Connecticut, though they would also
have a handsome apartment in New York. The vote had
definitely been taken: East Coast rather than West Coast.

While her husband was working on *Hud*, Joanne had not been idle. Motherhood — specifically, the birth of Melissa — hardly created an observable hiatus in her career, and in 1963, the year of *Hud*, her next picture, *The Stripper* (also known as *Woman Of Summer*), was released, too. If not in quite the same class as *Hud*, it should have done well, but it did not — perhaps because the studio, Fox, mistrusted their property and never gave it the support it needed. Failure of nerve (an important theme of *The Hustler*) has probably ruined as much artistic endeavour as failure of talent.

The *Stripper* was an adaptation of William Inge's play *A Loss Of Roses*, and while there were many reasons why Joanne should have found her role attractive, one of them must undoubtedly have been that the same dramatist's *Picnic* had in a sense brought Paul and her together and marked the true beginning of their careers roughly ten years earlier. Inge, who, sadly, was to commit suicide in the seventies, had been creatively associated with a string of films, usually adaptations of his own stage-plays. *Come Back, Little Sheba*, in 1953, was the first, to be followed three years later by *Picnic* and *Bus Stop*, both directed by Joshua Logan. The simultaneous appearance and success of the last two made Inge a hot property in Hollywood, which also grabbed *The Dark At The Top Of The Stairs* for filming in 1960, Harriet Frank and Irving Ravetch writing the screenplay. It was not all that surprising that Inge should be approached for an original work for the cinema, the result being the highly successful *Splendour In The Grass* (1961), directed by Elia Kazan, in which Warren Beatty made his début. The following year's *All Fall Down*, from a novel by James Leo Herlihy, also had a screenplay by William Inge that effectively explored a number of themes dear to his heart. At their best, his works were quietly and movingly revelatory, almost the dramatic antithesis of Tennessee Williams, who wrote of Inge, 'Bill and his work were suffused with the light of humanity at its best . . . he loved his characters, he wrote of them with a perfect ear for their homely speech, he saw them through their difficulties with the tenderness of a parent for suffering children. . . .'

The play *A Loss Of Roses* derives its title from the heroine's final acknowledgement of a harsh truth that seems, in retrospect, to have been before her even on her first day at school: 'I told Teacher I wanted back my roses. She shook her finger and said, when I gave away lovely presents, I couldn't expect to get them back. . . .' The play works out its theme to striking effect, but though for much of its length it follows the same story, *The Stripper* finally betrays the intentions of the original. The picture relates how ex-beauty-queen and Hollywood-reject Lila Green (Joanne) is stranded in her hometown, Salison in Kansas, when her lover and manager, Ricky (Robert Webber), disappears with the proceeds from the stage-show in which she has been appearing. Lila stays temporarily with Helen Baird (Claire Trevor), a widow who knew her years before but who shows concern when her teenage son Kenny (Richard Beymer in the role originally created on Broadway by Warren Beatty) has an affair with Lila. Conveniently for all others concerned — though scarcely for herself — Lila rejoins the sadistic Ricky, who is about to exploit her in a striptease-act. However, when Kenny sees the degrading display, he tells Lila that although he does not wish to marry her, he cares about her future and her happiness. Kenny's concern gives her the courage to part from Ricky and seek an independent life.

Probably as a result of her success in *Bus Stop*, the role of Lila had been intended for Marilyn Monroe, but it is unlikely that she would have done so well in it as Joanne, who had what Pauline Kael has called 'the right forlorn gallantry' for the part. Lila is a striking figure in Inge's gallery of ill-used innocents — a sister to Cherie in *Bus Stop* or Echo O'Brien (played by Eva Marie Saint) in *All Fall Down*. Without seeming to, Joanne dominates the film in a great performance, touchingly suggesting the tenderness and defencelessness of the heroine, and it is only in the closing sequences — when Lila, strengthened by Kenny's feelings, decides to be mistress of her fate — that she seems ill at ease. Not surprisingly. For the swift change of dramatic direction destroys the mood and thematic unity. Until these final, stridently melodramatic scenes, Meade Roberts' screenplay is excellent. Of course, *A Loss Of Roses* has no happy ending: Ricky turns up to take Lila off to her reluctant striptease-performance and taunts her, 'Where's the kid? I thought he'd be out here on a white horse to protect ya.' 'No,' Lila answers, 'No one's gonna proteck me.'

Franklin Schaffner, making his directorial début, handles his material with a nice feeling for subtle details of behaviour and with a sense of poetry. His vision of Lila, platinum-haired, arrayed in white, bathed in sunlight and lovingly observed by Ellsworth Fredericks's camera, seems to coincide exactly with Inge's, notably in a scene in which Lila talks to a neighbour's child and two different kinds of innocence tenderly combine.

Schaffner also gets a valuably credible performance from Richard Beymer, considerably better here than he was in *Adventures Of A Young Man*, as the callow yet oddly sympathetic boy, and as one of Inge's typical widows, Claire Trevor leaves an indelible impression of propriety and faintly neurotic concern. Jerry Goldsmith contributes an unobtrusive but effective score.

So much of the picture succeeds that its ending, arbitrarily stuck on to the story's natural conclusion, seems all the more shocking not only in its desertion of the dramatist's aims but also in its acquiescence to conventional sex-morality, happy-ending improbabilities and the come-on of the production's lurid title, Flawed *The Stripper* certainly is, but the defects are of a kind to arouse suspicion of front-office intervention, possible re-editing and the imposition of a 'positive' finale contrary to the director's wishes.

Nevertheless, it was arguably Joanne's best all-round film thus far — superior to *The Three Faces Of Eve* without being such an obvious showcase for her talents. Had its commercial success been greater, she would have had a great deal to be happy about. As things were, if, commercially, Paul was by that time on top of the world, then artistically the careers of *both* partners had reached an apogee.

8

Experiments And Failure

When Martin Ritt was a young actor in New York in the late
thirties, he made friends with John Garfield, and though Paul
Newman and Garfield had greater differences than
similarities, the Paul who attained pre-eminence in the years
1954–63 must have reminded Ritt in at least two ways of the
earlier star. To start with, there was the fact that Paul and
others in a new wave of moviestars had in a sense evolved from
a pattern that John Garfield had made familiar — that of the
doomed rebel, the loner embattled against overwhelming odds
or fighting a fierce struggle within himself. Through
Somebody Up There Likes Me and *The Hustler*, the public
had already begun associating Paul with such roles, and he
was to make them even more his own as the increasing
sombreness of his finest parts found its peak in *Cool Hand
Luke* and *Hombre*, in both of which he was to play doomed
heroes — losers in perhaps every worldly sense. (From one
viewpoint, even Hud Bannon may be seen as a loser.)

For anybody with a wide experience of moviegoing, the
Newman-Garfield points of similarity were focused sharply by
the closing sequence of *The Hustler* and Eddie Felson's
defiance of Bert Gordon and his threats. There is a strong
parallel with the last scene of Garfield's 1947 picture, *Body
And Soul*, — perhaps his greatest — which had the same
writer/director, Robert Rossen. As the fighter who has stayed
true to himself and to his talent and won the fight that the
mob expected him to throw, Garfield turns to villain Lloyd
Gough and says, 'What can you do — kill me? Everybody dies.'
It might be an earlier Eddie Felson speaking.

Ritt surely saw in Newman some of the qualities that he had
known in Garfield, both as man and star. To the later actor,
Ritt attributed 'a cool sexuality' together with 'an amused
quality and a high promise of danger', and by 1963, these
features had become stronger in Paul. Even though he lacked
the hard body of a Garfield, Paul had a fine physique, and

there was a tendency for him to play more physical roles that later films like *Winning, Cool Hand Luke* and *Harper* would underscore. Putting it another way, one might suggest that the vulnerability and spirituality of his earlier pictures had begun to recede — along with the intellectual qualities he had projected to make Anthony Judson Lawrence in *The Young Philadelphians* and Alfred Eaton in *From The Terrace* a persuasive lawyer and a convincing aeronautics engineer respectively. The great sensibility exhibited in *The Rack* and *Until They Sail* and even in episodes of *The Long Hot Summer* was to be seen more fitfully after *Hud* — subordinated to power, ruthlessness, ambition and other more conventionally masculine attributes. If this change was a loss, it was probably also inevitable in one who was now undoubtedly a superstar, *the* great phenomenon of the sixties.

In view of the decade, Paul's triumph was all the greater. The early sixties were a poor time for movies, and star after star, both new and old, failed to make the grade as television continued to keep audiences away from the cinema. But the clever promotional campaign for *Hud* had ubiquitously featured not only the phrase 'the man with the barbed-wire soul' (a description that appeared nowhere in the screenplay) but also the assertion 'Paul Newman *is Hud*'. True or false, the implication was that Paul was a personality-star of such magnitude that the public would flock to see *him* rather than the character he played or the picture he was in. Just as he was *Hud*, he was also to be *Harper, Hombre* and *Cool Hand Luke*. Three famous roles (the eponymous Lew Harper must be excluded) were to combine potently to fix once and for all the Newman persona. If Hud Bannon is the complete iconoclast, John Russell in *Hombre* is the total outcast and Luke in *Cool Hand Luke* is the intuitive rebel, the composite image is of the Great Loner. Before and since the mid sixties, Paul has played many different kinds of men, but the image cherished by his audience has not proved susceptible to real change.

He enjoyed his celebrity. No one can speculate meaningfully about what his career would have been had he stayed with Warners, but by tradition and in fact Warners was the studio of hustle, bustle and activity — determined, at least in the days of Jack Warner, to get the most out of its directors and stars, at the same time driving a hard bargain, as Paul had discovered, over salaries. For MGM, Paul had made *Sweet Bird Of Youth* for a breathtaking $350,000 plus a percentage, and his fee was rising. Having already made pictures for MGM, Fox, United Artists and Paramount, he enjoyed an enviable independence as one of the new breed of stars who made their own deals. With Martin Ritt, he formed a production-company, Jodell Productions (the title derived from syllables in the names of the two wives, Joanne and Adele). Much as Paul missed the stage and 'unprotected' acting, the theatre could be draining and a hard taskmaster, especially during a long run. After ten months of *Sweet Bird Of Youth* on Broadway, he described going to perform each night as 'like facing the dentist' — for all its rewards, an ordeal during which he would nightly lose three pounds.

But it was freedom and activity that Paul truly relished — not fame itself. He had appeared in little to be ashamed of and — dependent on who was doing the counting — in three or four or more first-rate films, with *Hud* the sort of achievement that most actors merely dreamed of. The fame that went with this sort of screen-exposure was another matter. He had never taken too kindly to being a sex-symbol — or perhaps more accurately, to being *merely* a sex-symbol. As for acting itself, there were times when he had little patience for the profession that had possibly chosen him as much as he had chosen it. 'It's silly, it's stupid,' he once said in a characteristic outburst, 'it has nothing whatever to do with being an adult.'

He had, of course, by no means cornered the market on such feelings, which are common among actors, particularly males, many of whom see or affect to see something unmanly in the business. For Paul, these periodic misgivings could be offset to some extent by his growing interest in high-powered cars and fast driving, which was to blossom by the seventies into participation in the unquestionably hairy sport of motor-racing. On the public highway, he would drive — with typical Newman hip understatement — an ordinary-looking Volkswagen beneath whose hood beats the mighty heart of a Porsche racing-engine.

After his new dimension of success and his third Academy

Award nomination, journalists still found him a tough subject to interview. In more ways than one. First, as jealous
of his privacy as ever, he would allow few encounters with
the gentlemen of the fourth estate, collaborating only grudg-
ingly when studio-publicists arranged such meetings and
tending to blend in protectively with the furniture and equip-
ment on the set. In public, the filmstar's inevitable dark
glasses preserved his anonymity to some degree, but he had
another trick all his own. He would slip a pencil, like a
horse's bit, between his teeth, and the unusual adornment
would serve to distort and — with luck — disguise features
that had become among the most familiar in the world.
Second, however, Paul caused problems for interviewers
by being extremely laconic. His verbal meagreness was no
pose, but rather an inability to dish up smart, glib answers,
to supply the crisp superficialities that are the staple fare
of the interviewing ritual. By this time, he was becoming
notorious for the long pause that would follow when he
was asked a direct question, the disappointing and unhelpful 'Yes' or 'No', the reply that began promisingly only to
crumble in a sentence that tailed away. For his part, Paul
complained about the solemnity of some of the questions
he was asked — predictable and tiresome inquiries about the
Method, for example. A large part of the truth was that
he bore enduring scars from his early years when the press
had insisted on comparing him with Brando, cynically reluctant to allow a rising star his own identity and uniqueness.

     In the eyes of the world — or at least the critical section
of it — attaining such heights imposes as many obligations
as privileges, and a superstar, blessed with freedom of choice,
must select his roles with care and discrimination. So ran
the thinking that led many to condemn the next development
in Paul's career, and on the evidence of his three pictures
following *Hud*, the judgement is not easy to refute, however
simple it may be to explain the nature of Paul's failure.
Truism though it may be, the general observation should
be borne in mind that masterpieces are not plucked out
of a hat: a star, however powerful, may choose only from
the scripts available. Then there were at least two other
factors that might have led Paul astray — besides, that is,

any actor's thirst for novelty, his desire to appear in something that promises, perhaps falsely, to be different. He still wished to score a hit as a light comedian, and he was also anxious that he and Joanne, co-starring, should have the unqualified success that had so far eluded them. If a trio of disappointing films could not be excused by these twin impulses, they at least help to clarify what might otherwise seem unperceptive choices.

The first was *A New Kind Of Love*, which found Paul once again co-starring with Joanne and once more essaying farcical comedy. What he expected to accomplish with such a script is conjectural, but the result was fairly disastrous — a limp but hefty (110 minutes) package that included a sophomore's view of Paris and, for Joanne, the overworked ugly-duckling-into-swan routine, after which transformation the plot had Paul mistake her for a prostitute. Melville Shavelson, who wrote, produced and directed, had revealed a fecund and professional talent in the past, especially for witty one-liners, but *A New Kind Of Love* was the old kind of farcical error over which it is kindest to draw a veil. If Paul and Joanne were to be blamed, it was only for endorsing with their participation so hopeless an enterprise. Their playing, alert and sensitive as ever, could do little with the material. The critics who said that Paul Newman had failed yet again in comedy, however, were wrong, for he had yet to be tried. When a man's feet and wrists are bound, only a fool blames him for his inability to swim.

The Prize, a thriller set in Stockholm during the week of the Nobel Prize ceremonies, was considerably better, even if it was obvious imitation Hitchcock that fell far short of the real thing. Ernest Lehman, who had scripted both Paul's *Somebody Up There Likes Me* and Hitchcock's masterly *North By Northwest*, had provided a fair-to-good screenplay, and Mark Robson, who managed to accomplish little with the intractable stuff of *From The Terrace* (also written by Lehman), did considerably better with the later film, which even on paper must have looked decidedly more promising than the previous Newman-Lehman-Robson collaboration. Nevertheless, *The Prize* has a tired, *déjà-vu* aura. The admixture of thrills, comedy and action that can seem so smooth and easy in Hitchcock is a difficult chemistry to regulate successfully, and it fails to cohere to good effect in this picture. There is a familiar Hitchcockian theme — the reluctant involvement of a (relatively) ordinary citizen in extraordinary, not to say criminal, events; and Lehman in essence reprises a famous sequence from *North By Northwest* (in which, in order to get himself protectively arrested, Cary Grant creates a disturbance at an auction) by inserting a parallel scene in *The Prize* during which Paul, clad only in a towel, interrupts a nudist conference with the similar aim of having himself rescued by Swedish police from pursuing hoodlums. Paul is as good as his lines allow him to be, but it is not without significance that he is at his best when he is permitted a cutting edge — notably in the sequence that depicts his arrival at Stockholm Airport, where he is virtually poured off the plane and counters his onslaught by a previously neglectful world-press with the sardonic inquiry: 'Where were you when I needed you?' (Paul Newman himself might be speaking.) His role — that of a somewhat drunken, disillusioned author — lacks the depth necessary for even this type of movie. Cary Grant could have coruscated over the thin ice; Paul cannot quite bring off the feat. In general, failure is easier to analyse than success, but of *The Prize* one can say only that despite Stockholm locations, a brilliant score by Jerry Goldsmith and a valiant effort from a starry cast that includes Edward G. Robinson, Diane Baker and Elke Sommer, the picture never takes fire and is instead an agreeable but undemanding (here, perhaps, lies the failure) example of a difficult genre.

The choice of film might be wondered at, but Paul's involvement in *What A Way To Go!*, released in 1964, though amounting to little more than a guest-shot, could not be faulted. The picture has been rather unfairly slandered by critics quick to spot its unhappy combination of slightness of plot and inflation of treatment. The story concerns an unambitious, unmaterialistic girl (Shirley MacLaine) who marries a series of happy-go-lucky men, each of whom destroys himself, making her a widow, through largely involuntary success. In his own episode, Paul, one of five big male stars, plays a Parisian artist who devises a painting-machine that is actuated by music. At the height of his aesthetic and worldly triumph, the machine turns on him and devours him. His performance is excellent, richly comic, especially when he speaks in French with witty English sub-titles. But by Newman standards, this feat is small beer and creates the impression of a great actor amusing himself through five-finger exercises. In itself, his playing is entertainingly admirable. But he appears to be taking a holiday that can only disappoint his admirers.

Three movies in a row that, if they did no lasting harm, tended to blur his star-image must have been a matter of concern to Paul, who had probably expected more from all of them. Nor, after *A New Kind Of Love*, was Joanne doing any better. She appeared in the now almost totally forgotten *Signpost To Murder*, which had little to commend it. One commentator said that her participation in so inept and old-fashioned a venture implied 'that she had despaired of getting good offers'.

Paul, on the other hand, thought he had a marketable property in *The Outrage*, for which he joined forces for the fifth time with Martin Ritt. The cash-paying customers, however, said differently. The choice of subject *was* somewhat strange — a Michael Kanin script based on the play by Fay and Michael Kanin, in turn based on Kurosawa's famous film *Rashomon*. 'What is truth?' *Rashomon* had asked in its laboriously intellectual way, and the cold cerebration, the flavour of a mechanical philosophical exercise, is present in *The Outrage*, too, though it comes nowhere near answering the question. Geography and chronology are revised to remove the story from eighth-century Japan to late nineteenth-century Southwestern US, but Ritt and cameraman James Wong Howe, who makes Texas palpable in *Hud*, fail to establish the action in any really tangible setting. To prepare for his role as Juan Carrasco, the Mexican bandit originally played on Broadway by Rod Steiger, Paul spent two weeks in Mexico, studying language and customs, and though he had had a Bohemian beard in *What A Way To Go!*, this time his beard was scruffy and unkempt, his disguise heightened by dark contact lenses and a false nose.

In the story, Carrasco is convicted of raping a woman

(Claire Bloom, who took the same role in the play) and murdering her husband (Laurence Harvey). Though the rape is not in doubt, its exact circumstances vary according to which of the four people involved in the plot is telling the story, and the four versions related in the film present the death of the husband in markedly differing ways. The picture's mood and the styles of acting fluctuate wildly, though all the players have their moments. Moments, however, are not enough, and the drama never comes convincingly to life.

Anybody sympathetic to Paul Newman will try hard to find virtues in his acting in *The Outrage*, in which he himself considered he gave his best performance, but the attempt, if not doomed to failure, is a daunting one. He certainly seems Mexican and uncouth, but the playing lacks variation and subtlety and ultimately may be seen as a *tour de force* in the true, slightly arid sense — a technical feat that is deeply involved in the use of make-up, verbal modification and physical mannerisms.

Paul at first thought the role unplayable, at least by him, and took it on as a challenge. His assessment might have been shrewder than he knew. No matter how successful Rod Steiger's portrayal had been in the theatre, Juan Carrasco was possibly a character who, regardless of any actor's advocacy, would simply not find acceptance on the screen; for as Laurence Olivier once said, 'I'm quite shocked to find how exaggerated stage-acting is after the films. I simply didn't notice it before, but now it seems to me that in the theatre audiences swallow dialogue and acting-conventions which on the screen would draw howls of derisive laughter.'

(For his part, Rod Steiger had said of the Carrasco-role, 'If an actor stays on one level and doesn't challenge himself constantly, he will die. That's why I was eager to do *Rashomon*.')

One can see what Paul hoped the movie would accomplish for him, how he believed that here was a chance to demonstrate his versatility and escape from the stereotype of the star. Indeed, attempting such a role illustrated the fact that Paul Newman was courageously different from those stars who played safe by repeating virtually the same role in picture after picture. Nevertheless, the cool, not to say hostile, reception of *The Outrage* was a depressing business.

The gloom, however, was not unrelieved, for on 14th April 1964, the Newmans opened in a success at the Little Theatre, New York — the play *Baby Want A Kiss*, an off-Broadway production presented by the Actors' Studio. In effect, the label 'Actors' Studio presentation' meant that Paul and Joanne were each taking just over one hundred dollars a week and that the Studio would benefit — Paul's idea, perhaps, of discharging a little of his debt to the body that had, by his own admission, done so much for his artistic development. The play was directed by Frank Corsaro and written by James Costigan, a friend of the Newmans to whom Joanne had once been engaged. Costigan also played one of the roles.

For both Paul and Joanne — all too used to the problems of concentrating on a film-characterization built up in short takes during which studio-lights glared at them and there were distracting, half-perceived movements on the periphery of the set — it was an enormous and salutary stimulus to experience again interaction with a live audience whose responses would inspire and immediately reward the actors on the stage. However, mindful of the other side of the coin, the deadening effect of long-run plays, Paul committed them only to a four-month engagement. Not surprisingly in view of the casting of two such stars, tickets sold heavily.

After *Sweet Bird Of Youth*, Paul had read hundreds of plays without finding anything arresting until he studied Costigan's two-act comedy, which contained provocative ideas as well as humour. The theme was the perhaps overexploited one of the Hollywood couple whose public front of blissful domesticity is revealed to mask bitter antipathy. With the status of Paul and Joanne and their own reputation as a golden pair, it might have been thought that the production had an element of teasing, that the Newmans had their tongues just slightly in their cheeks. John Chapman of the *New York Daily News* touched on this aspect of the proceedings when he suggested that the play was 'more fun for those who are in it than those who are at it'. The work garnered some aloof and mistrustful reviews, but the playing of the Newmans was generally praised, even in Walter Kerr's otherwise austere notice for the *New York Herald Tribune*. For the second time in his career, though the problems of Brick in *Cat On A Hot Tin Roof* had been far from clear in the film-version, Paul played a character with strong homosexual traits — a fact that would be scarcely worth mentioning had such an undertaking still not required a modicum of courage in 1964. As it was, many people in the audience, both critics and ordinary playgoers, found acutely distasteful the scene in which Paul proposed to the old friend played by Costigan.

After the play had closed, the Newman screen-career resumed in August when he left for Europe to make *Lady L*, in which he would co-star with Sophia Loren — a teaming that had been earlier announced for a screen-version, never made, of Arthur Miller's *After The Fall*. The pedigree of *Lady L* was curious and was to become even stranger. In the late fifties, MGM had acquired the rights of Romain Gary's novel with the intention of filming it with Tony Curtis and Gina Lollobrigida as stars, but the project was dropped, only to be revived in 1964 when Newman and Loren contracted to appear and Peter Ustinov agreed to direct, also writing the screenplay. (Much earlier, George Cukor had been announced as a possible director, and actually began work in 1961 with Lollobrigida and Curtis). Paul was to celebrate his fortieth birthday on the set of *Lady L* in Paris, but the picture was finished three months later in April, 1965, its last location being at Castle Howard, England, in particularly inhospitable weather. Clearly — and perhaps not surprisingly — MGM lacked confidence in the film, and though it was shown in Europe later in the year, premièring in London that November, its release was delayed in New York until May of the following year — in fact, after Paul's next film, *Harper*, had been shown. Such a postponement had never before been inflicted on a Paul Newman picture, and the auguries were not good. If it had been hoped that *Lady L* might in some way cash in on the success of *Harper*, the optimistic thinking was doomed to disappointment, and *Lady L* proved a flop that has rarely been shown since.

Overlong at 124 minutes, the picture fails to be the light, charming vehicle as which it was no doubt intended. The story is told to her biographer by the eighty-year-old Lady Lendale (Sophia Loren) and depicts her life of sexual conquest and revolutionary involvement—the second through her true-love, the anarchist Armand (Paul). When Armand is in danger from the police, Lord Lendale (David Niven) offers to save him if Louise, as she then is, will become Lady Lendale. She agrees, and there begins a strange *ménage à trois*, with Lady Lendale a bigamist, Armand her chauffeur and, in the end, eight children bearing the Lendale name but actually Armand's progeny. A period piece, full of well-intentioned eccentricities, *Lady L* is quite pretty to look at but devoid of pronounced flair or style, Peter Ustinov's delicate, affectionate touch lacking the bold strokes that might have saved it. Urbane and civilized, David Niven steals the picture.

As for Paul, he had observably improved: the critical consensus that he was 'hopelessly miscast' in *The Outrage* changed to the verdict that in *Lady L* he was merely 'miscast'. Wisely, he had relied heavily on the Newman charm, certainly not misplaced in this context, and it had seen him through.

More or less.

Overall, things had not been going too well. Fortunately, though, life was not just movies, and there were what George in *Who's Afraid Of Virginia Woolf?* calls 'compensations'.

In April, long before *Lady L* was shown there, the writer Rona Jaffe saw Paul and a very pregnant Joanne at their apartment in New York. Unaided, Joanne cooked and served a connoisseur's dinner. Afterwards, while Paul and Miss Jaffe sat in the living-room discussing the state of the theatre, Joanne went upstairs to concentrate on her condition.

The next morning, 21st April, she gave birth to a third daughter, Claire.

9

Top of the World

Paul Newman at forty was an actor of enviably wide accomplishment. He had worked extensively in live television before film removed much of the spontaneity from the medium, and the discipline and pressure of a perpetual opening night had given him the experience otherwise to be provided only by repertory theatre. In the theatre itself, he had learned how to build and sustain a performance, to keep up the immense concentration required. Films, on the other hand, had taught him a different kind of concentration—how to hang on to the concept of a character for a mere three minutes at a time, how to keep hold of the thread of psychological continuity during out-of-sequence shooting. As a star, he had faced up to responsibility and the myriad pressures of Hollywood. Having known commercial and artistic failure as well as success, he had learned how to roll with the punches, how to avoid that crumbling of nerve that can bedevil the career of any artist.

Behind him were years of solid achievement. His popularity was phenomenal, even though there had been changes of direction that comparatively few understood, as well as the failures with which even fewer sympathized. Deliberately and repeatedly, he had returned to the theatre—both to refresh himself and to put his talent to the test. By this time, he knew well that in the movies a strong, photogenic personality could be made to look uncannily like an actor, and he wanted more than the surface-appearance of histrionic gifts.

If an actor's chief aims are prestige, money and satisfaction, Paul had abundantly claimed the first two, and any qualification applicable to his satisfaction had more to do with the divine discontent of the artist than with the frustration of a performer realistically assessing his potential and his past interpretations.

Enviably, his looks now showed maturity without age—a

state of affairs that most men merely dreamed about or, in legend, made pacts with the devil to obtain. He had the physique of one in his twenties, took a daily sauna and exercised regularly, specializing in push-ups. Though he continued to eat frugally, he was still a hefty beer-drinker, but he easily burned up what he consumed.

If anything, by the age of forty, Paul's inclination towards reserve in public- and semi-public settings had intensified. During interviews, he persisted in taking time to think before answering questions — often to dignify a stupid inquiry with a half-way sensible reply. On the set, fierce in his concentration, he was virtually unapproachable, but crews and fellow cast-members would respect his instinct for privacy. His sense of humour tended to be offbeat and bizarre — esoteric even to Joanne.

To his six children, he was a good father, and despite the doomsayers of Hollywood, the Newman marriage continued to flourish. It thrived on many ingredients, not least a rare honesty that spilled over into professional activity. Each regarded the other as an ultimate authority on their performances, and Paul said once, 'We respect each other tremendously, and if one of us criticises the other, the criticism is taken as gospel.' Their differences continued to be complementary rather than divisive, but like all couples, they had their big disagreements, and if these were sometimes fiery and emotional, Paul's view was that a big blow-up cleared or sweetened the air.

An inability to find commercially sound properties with strong parts for both of them unquestionably inhibited their professional partnership, and the imbalance of popular regard had its irritations, at least for Joanne. If Paul's sex-symbol status became wearying to him, it was more a provocation to his wife, especially the public manifestations of it. During the run of *Baby Want A Kiss*, Joanne had hated being elbowed aside by the screaming girls who would mob her husband, and as the years went by, being cast as Mrs Paul Newman grew no less irksome to Joanne, whose own sense of identity demanded the recognition that she was not only an individual person but also an artist of great attainment. Being elbowed aside was almost symbolic — hence her reaction. For the fans of a male superstar, a wife was an inconvenient irrelevance.

After her two-year absence from the screen, Joanne needed a good picture for her return, both to erase the failure of *Signpost To Murder* and to remind people, if their memories were short, of how fine an actress she was. What she got was not one good picture but two; and the first, even if she did not have a conventional star-role, was superb — an eccentric and serious comedy. Irvin Kershner's *A Fine Madness* allowed her a rich character-study as Rhoda Shillitoe, wife of the Dionysiac poet Samson Shillitoe (Sean Connery), and though she was offscreen for much of the time, she nevertheless registered strongly in a part that revealed endearingly what Pauline Kael has called her 'likeable "trouper" quality'. Released in the same year, 1966, *A Big Hand For The Little Lady* (also known as *Big Deal At Dodge City*) was not quite in the same class, having been inflated from a forty-eight minute teleplay by Sidney Carroll into a ninety-six minute motion picture. In contrast to her tattered and battered appearance as Rhoda Shillitoe, Joanne's looks were allowed to be seen at their loveliest, and it was an amusing in-joke that the script should require so spirited a person to simulate, as part of an elaborate confidence-trick, helpless femininity. In a distinguished cast, Robert Middleton, Jason Robards, Kevin McCarthy and Charles Bickford were the four poker-players fittingly but disastrously smitten with her beauty. Neither film created a sensation, but both benefited from Joanne's stunningly good acting.

On the other hand, Paul's next picture did better than it deserved, becoming a smash-hit that brought his career out of the doldrums created by works such as *The Outrage* and *Lady L*. For *Harper* (also known as *The Moving Target*), he returned after a seven-year interval to Warner Brothers, where he was photographed smiling during rehearsals in the company of an equally affable Jack Warner — 'proof' of an uneasy reconciliation. What made the reunion possible, however, was not unconnected with the $750,000 Paul was now getting against ten per cent of the gross. *Harper* would also put him back among the first ten at the box-office in 1966.

In some ways, *Harper* was first-rate: it was a fairly stylish high-budget production that looked as though, with luck, it might revive the P.I. genre that had been at its height in the mid forties with the filming of Raymond Chandler's *The Big Sleep*; its timing was right; it came about as close as might have been expected in the jaded sixties to taking itself with the appropriate degree of seriousness; and it offered a corrective to all those boringly indestructible espionage-heroes and that stodgy diet of semi-parody in which Derek Flint and Matt Helm had been the only aspirants to panache and elegance. Unfortunately, however, there was also a great deal amiss with *Harper* — notably, Jack Smight's sluggish direction, the thinness of most of the characterization, and a knowing, arch quality in a William Goldman screenplay that was witty without coruscating.

More than a decade later, the movie starts and ends well, but in between there is variable, unequal material that is uncertainly handled. In a performance modelled on both Bogart and Robert Kennedy, Paul strives valiantly to inject into the film a moral force that is sadly missing. His Harper has a sardonic toughness, excellently appropriate, that is to be found in the script, but, unsupported by the writing, Paul's characterization also conveys hints of a redeeming sensibility. The opening sequence, during which, having discovered he is out of coffee, Harper shudderingly retrieves yesterday's grounds from the trash-can, epitomizes the humanity of the classic screen P.I., who is unglamorous, fallible, vulnerable, an improviser who takes his women and his liquor where he finds them — and not without finer feelings. Harper, the star's acting suggests, is a casualty, and he has compassion for other casualties as he pursues his investigation through the traditionally involved plot. His feral instincts and cynical opportunism are more than adequately catered for by Goldman's lines, but as Paul Newman plays him, Harper knows only too well weakness and the noble, stupid, craven tricks of the heart. There are fascinating overtones of tragedy in a unique exchange during which Harper deliberately vilifies Julie Harris in the presence of Robert Wagner, who is supposed not to know her, until Wagner, tears in his eyes, draws a gun on the detective and in so doing betrays himself as her lover and accomplice. The depth of the scene stems from Paul's small signs that he hates what he has to do and finds Wagner's self-destructive gallantry his noblest feature. Belatedly, the script, too, gives Harper moral scruples, so that when the detective looks as though he will hand over to the law his murdering friend (Arthur Hill), higher principles prevail, he mutters, 'Aw, hell!', and he is in the act of shrugging as the film's last frame freezes. Paul puts a great effort into these closing moments, but it cannot entirely erase impressions created earlier of genuine nastiness. The star's vision and the writer's do not coincide, but there can be no doubt about whose is the more attractive: Harper's better self strives to emerge through Paul's first-rate acting.

One bit of 'stunt'-casting backfired badly. The inclusion of Lauren Bacall among the players served only as a reminder that Jack Smight was no Howard Hawks and *Harper* no *Big Sleep* — the film in which Bacall had co-starred most romantically and most effectively with Humphrey Bogart.

Harper was the second of three big and popular Newman films (the third being *Hombre*) whose titles began with the same letter. A story circulated that Paul's manager wanted the three *H*'s as a publicity-gimmick. The facts are uncertain, but it is true that Ross Macdonald's detective in his novel *The Moving Target*, upon which *Harper* is based, is called Lew Archer and that there was no other apparent reason for the change to Lew Harper.

If *Harper* was no *Big Sleep*, then *Torn Curtain*, released in the same year, was no *Harper*. The lure of working with the legendary Alfred Hitchcock had proved so great that Paul accepted his role without having studied Brian Moore's script. He should have made the time, for it was thin, unpromising stuff. Furthermore, Hitchcock and his star were temperamentally worlds apart, achieving their artistic ends by quite disparate means, and the director, in interviews with François Truffaut, later voiced his dissatisfaction with the way Paul acted in the picture. Nevertheless, a different approach would have made minimal improvement. The plot, about an apparently defecting atomic scientist (But he's played by Paul Newman, so how can he be what he seems?), is wafer-thin, despite its twists and turns, and Brian Moore, no Ernest Lehman, creates characters that lack life and credibility. Paul's co-star is Julie Andrews, and publicity for *Torn Curtain* took the crudely predictable line of nudging potential customers about the scandalous delight of finding Mary Poppins and the screen's great lover in bed together. In fact, the Andrews-Newman chemistry worked little better than its Newman-Hitchcock counterpart.

(In any case, it is an interesting if little remarked upon point that Paul has enjoyed his greatest successes through playing men without women — a state of affairs that may have much to do with his popularity the world over, since females in his audience may thus respond to him without feeling the threat of competition on the screen, unconsciously and intuitively offering the star *their* comfort, *their* understanding and *their* admiration. In *The Hustler*, Sarah dies, and Eddie Felson is left alone. Hud's girls are fleeting diversions, and he is essentially solitary. Lew Harper is divorced and similarly a loner. In *Hombre* and *Cool Hand Luke*, two outstanding successes that were just around the corner, he would play characters devoid of any strong attachment to particular women — even if the emotional side of John Russell in *Hombre* is more complicated than it might seem; and in one of his most famous films, *Butch Cassidy And The Sundance Kid*, Paul would play yet again a man lacking any central sexual-tie.)

Torn Curtain was not a happy experience for Paul Newman, and in retrospect it became a film that he disowned, even though it proved a bigger commercial hit than *Harper*. But just as failure tends to alienate people, success makes everybody friends, and the full team of Newman, director Martin Ritt and writers Ravetch and Frank, having rung the bell resoundingly with *The Long Hot Summer* and *Hud*, joined forces once more for *Hombre*. It was to turn out, however, only a moderate commercial success, perhaps because it mystified critics and public in two ways — either of them sufficient to prevent its being an out-and-out hit. First, its depth and subtlety were such that it gave up comparatively little at first viewing. Second, in a world where labels count for more than they should, it was an unusual, possibly even unique, Western that eschewed the conventional patterns and clichés of the genre.

Nevertheless, *Hombre* must be a strong nomination for Paul's best picture, and if the receipts disappointed, the explanation lay partly, it might have been presumed, in the fact that the star was again claiming a versatility that his public was not prepared to allow him.

Paul's preliminary research and study for his role followed a by-then familiar pattern. Since the ways and manners of Indians were important to his characterization, he visited a reservation to observe them, his attention specially drawn by one man who stood for an hour without moving, his foot tucked up behind him, and simply watched what was happening in the street. 'I stole that stance for *Hombre*', Paul said later. The part was to be the most laconic he ever played, and yet, for all its lack of words, it is one of his most eloquent, haunting roles.

Despite its considerable ramifications, the plot of *Hombre* is a simple but brutal variation on the classic Guy de Maupassant 'Boule de Suif' situation, but it admirably serves writers and director as a framework for the painstaking delineation of character and the exploration of such themes as racism and human need and responsibility. On a dangerous journey, John Russell (Paul) is the slighted, socially ostracized figure, a character more Apache than white man, who turns out to be the most needed and valuable member of the party. However, he proves himself a complete loner and is moved to save the life of a worthless fellow-traveller (Barbara Rush again, after eight years) only when Jessie (Diane Cilento), whom he admires, is herself about to make the attempt, Russell has also taken the money a criminal gang were after in the hold-up of the stage-coach on which most of the characters have been travelling — money that has been stolen from his own tribe by a corrupt Indian-agent (Fredric March). Though the other passengers on the trip misinterpret actions that Russell is too aloof to explain, his one aim is to return the money to the Apaches.

The story is a parable on at least two levels. Russell's character, his asceticism, his incorruptibility, his self-sufficiency, remind us that America is the land of Thoreau ('Our life is frittered away by detail. . . . Simplicity, simplicity, simplicity!'). On another level, the superior white race is decidedly on trial in *Hombre*, and when Russell's motives are finally revealed, Ritt succeeds admirably in recording the expressions — a touching mixture of shame and amazement — of those who have misjudged the man by assessing his conduct in terms of their own squalid instincts or cynical philosophies. One exchange epitomizes both themes. 'You'll see,' says the Indian-agent. 'White folks stick together.' Russell laconically counters, 'They better.'

Paul's role is described by Pauline Kael at her most perceptive: 'Split in his loyalties, the half-and-half hero can observe the cruelties and misunderstandings of both sides; he's a double loner — an ideally alienated, masochistic modern hero.' So assimilated into the tribe that has reared him, Russell at least begins with no loyalties to the whites, and thus the part is not readily understood without also taking into account the key-role of Jessie. On the one hand, she can say of marriage, 'It's the price you pay if you want it where you can nudge it in the night.' On the other, it is she who makes the picture's articulate humanitarian plea: 'We'd better deal with each other out of need, not merit — because none of us have too much of that.' Ironically, her words are wasted on Russell, this arresting embodiment of Thoreau's 'simple and independent' mind; it is only when she threatens to put her own life in jeopardy that he moves forward to take her place, thus, out of love, acting according to Jessie's merit rather than Audra Favor's (Barbara Rush) need. A neat paradox.

Unless one counts *Hud* (and some commentators, oddly, did), *Hombre* is Ritt's first Western, and it is interesting to observe how he handles the genre's violence. Almost arbitrarily, and all the more shockingly as a result, it flares up without warning. Nowhere is it more disturbing and intense than in the sequence in which Russell tackles the bandit who has been taunting two Apaches. Almost casually, Russell steps up to the man, then, striking like a snake, jerks a rifle-butt damagingly into his face and mutters unemotionally, 'No more, huh?' These tense, brief explosions are balanced by more poetic sequences such as the near-rhapsodic, sensitively edited opening in which Russell and his Apaches are trapping horses, a beginning that is an accurate augury of the assurance Ritt manifests throughout the film. Though the overall tempo is one of Brucknerian reflectiveness, there are no mistakes of pace here, and the images are marvellously selected and captured by James Wong Howe's colour camerawork.

In the beautifully written role of Jessie — splendidly the natural woman, with a beguiling mixture of delicacy and earthiness — Diane Cilento gives a staggeringly good performance. (One suspects that the character might originally have been conceived for Patricia Neal.) The part is balanced by those of the two other females, perverted, antipathetic creatures as they are, Barbara Rush making a strong impression as the frigid, calculating wife of Fredric March, who himself contributes one of his best sketches of bigotry and hypocrisy. In an histrionically distinguished picture, Martin Balsam and Frank Silvera are also excellent, while, as Cicero Grimes, Richard Boone makes a redoubtable bad man. One of Ritt's haunting images is of Grimes struggling to his feet to attack Russell — a wounded, savage bear shambling towards death.

Even so, the film belongs to Newman. He stands, sits and moves with the tidiness of impeccable physical discipline. In a superb study of dignity and hauteur, those pellucid blue eyes now challenge, now mock, now soften subtly with humour or pity. Nothing is wasted. And Ritt, mindful of the picture's title, gives him a fitting death — swift, unlucky, but the end of a man whose courage and integrity are at an apogee. His qualities are celebrated by the two mourning, at last comprehending figures of Diane Cilento and Martin Balsam, whom Wong Howe's camera leaves to dwell in visual threnody on the calm, stoical features of Russell, magnificent in death, until the director, in a manner somewhat like that of George Stevens in *Giant*, dissolves on a still photograph of the tragically depleted and wronged race who reared 'hombre' — the most grave and reverent images Ritt has so far left for us to brood upon.

For much of the film, Paul simply *is* — though its closing sequences compel him into the kind of action most commonly associated with a star. Even then, however, his deeds call for an uncommon amount of thought from audiences. So soft and sentimental are our conceptions about humanity — especially humanity personified by a superstar — that John Russell's attitude and conduct seem for more than two-thirds of the film's length incredibly, unforgivably callous. But *Hombre* will have no truck with traditional heroics or *macho* displays. It is a brave, underrated picture that shows Paul's acting at its most intelligent and Ritt's mastery of his subject at its most complete.

The demands of the film might have proved baffling for the main body of Newman fans and consequently reduced takings. At the same time, however, it seems safe to say that those same fans, even if they were unaware of it, probably had an *intuitive* understanding of the character of John Russell that did the star's popularity no harm at all.

Could you beat *Hombre?* Well, yes — in commercial terms, you certainly could. And Paul followed the picture with what many continue to think his finest movie.

Cool Hand Luke had a screenplay written by Donn Pearce and Frank Pierson from the former's novel, and it was a film that knew exactly what it was about, even if it played straight into the hands of those who saw masochism, death-wishes, rebellion and martyrdom in the archetypal Paul Newman role. (Involuntary or deliberate, the exploration of such territory was of course highly profitable.) To those who point out — or invent — the Newman trademarks, two observations should be made: the character of Luke was taken over from the parent-novel, which was presumably written without Paul in mind at all; and such episodes as physical beatings can occur and recur *by chance* in the career of a star. (To adduce one significant argument, those who categorize the star-persona of, say, Brando as masochistic overlook those inconvenient and numerically superior roles in which the actor undergoes no physical punishment at all.) The debate is not about the beatings or the deaths of the characters played by Paul; it is, rather, about the *emphasis* placed on these facets not so much by movie-makers or their public as by a coterie of critics.

Cool Hand Luke, the story of a misfit who becomes a shackled prisoner in a southern state, escapes repeatedly and is at last mortally wounded — only to become a mythical figure to his fellow-prisoners, is worked out with a remarkable consistency, even though the beauty of some of the film's images is occasionally self-conscious and factitious. The picture of Luke is one of near-total alienation. He may be unable to relate to the outside world, but his relationship with the other inmates is more an accommodation than genuine feeling. Since solitary confinement is his natural state, it is not solitary confinement that breaks him but exhaustion produced by constant and systematic brutality. It is hard to see what else could await him but death, and thus his fate has a tragic inevitability.

More so than any other character played by Paul, Luke is the complete loner: he lives and dies without a dime or a woman or a friend. Even the superficially warm relationship between him and another convict, Dragline (George Kennedy), is a slightly one-sided affair, and with a certainty not unlike Ari Ben Canaan's conviction of Jewish isolation in *Exodus*, he knows well that when the chips are down, he will stand alone. In a finely managed scene, Paul makes the point with anguish and economy. After he has been broken into submission by physical debility, his fellow-convicts, to whom he has previously been a hero, turn from him. 'Where are you?' Luke cries, unanswerably. 'Where are you *now*?' He is strong — sustained and nourished by his own spirit, though it is not inexhaustible, and he can become angry about others' dependence on him, their habit of sensing his power and feeding on it.

At the beginning of the film, Paul conveys with appropriately insolent ease the coolness that prompts the character's soubriquet. A floorwalker (guard) observes his mocking smile and says with weary presentiment, 'I hope you ain't gonna be a hard case.' Later, the sadistic camp-boss (Strother Martin) peevishly complains, 'What we've got here is a failure to communicate. Some men you just can't reach.' But Paul projects Luke's defiance, his inability to bow his head, with an almost philosophical restraint that is far removed from the cockiness of Ben Quick or Rocky Graziano.

The performance is never solemn or sober, but infused, on the contrary, with humanity and humour. Nevertheless,

the star conveys with enviable control Luke's growing fatigue
—a spiritual weakening whose gradual development is impli-
cit in Paul's quiet but perfect articulation of such lines as:
'I done enough world-shakin' for a while. . . .'

When Luke is visited by his mother, Arletta (Jo van Fleet),
two great talents formidably sustain a long, understated
scene—their only one in the film. After Arletta has talked
of approaching death and her abandoned hope of seeing
Luke 'well fixed' before she goes, Paul injects into the man's
words his sad acceptance of his own intransigence and a
sense of his longing for release: 'A man's got to go his own
way. . . . I tried to live always free and above board like
you, but I don't know—I just can't seem to find no elbow-
room.'

Paul handles magnificently two key-scenes. The first occurs
after Luke has been told of Arletta's death. He expresses
and simultaneously conquers his grief by picking up his banjo
and starting to sing—at first faltering and on the point of
complete breakdown and then with mounting assurance
and serenity, to the words: 'I don't care if it rains or freezes,/
'Long as I got my plastic Jesus. . . .' ·

The climax of the film calls for even greater control and
the ability to mould and shape a performance. Free once
more, Luke stumbles into a deserted church in which, in
a speech that might have defeated a lesser actor, he addres-
ses himself to the Almighty: 'I know I'm a pretty evil fellow.
I killed people in the war, and I got drunk and chewed
up municipal property and the like. I know I got no call
to ask too much, but even so you got to admit you ain't
dealt me no cards in a long time. It's beginning to look
like you got things fixed so I cain't never win out. Besides,
I'm tired of all them rules and regulations and bosses. You
made me like I am. The thing is—where am I supposed
to fit in? Old man, I gotta tell you. I started out pretty
strong and fast. But it's beginning to get to me. Just when
does it end? What have you got in mind for me? What
do I do now? . . . I guess I gotta find my own way.'

Paul handles this veritable outsider's credo or paean to
alienation with the skill and authority of a master. What
should be in the speech—self-mockery, amused resignation,

gravity, courage and stoicism — *is* there; what might have been ruinous — self-pity, whining, facile emotionalism — is utterly absent.

One may have reservations about *Cool Hand Luke*, the film — excellent though it generally is and expertly directed by Stuart Rosenberg. But there need be no reservations about Paul's performance. It is the assured, sensitive work of one who is much more than well cast.

Luke was perhaps his most demanding role physically since *Somebody Up There Likes Me*: he fights with gloves on, he shovels dirt, he runs, he jumps fences and leaps streams. He went to West Virginia for considerable preparation that included accustoming himself to walking and running in shackles.

The film was shot on location at the San Joaquin River Delta. On hand both to ensure authenticity and to act a bit-role himself was Donn Pearce, whose novel had been to some extent based on experience, for Pearce was a former safecracker who had known imprisonment at first hand. (Some years later, Milos Forman was to have an enormous success by turning into a film Ken Kesey's novel *One Flew Over The Cuckoo's Nest* — a book whose storyline, though the action is set in a mental institution, has strong similarities to *Cool Hand Luke* that went entirely unremarked. The later picture, a hit for Jack Nicholson, proved nothing else so strongly as that a youthful audience could still be hooked by the familiar, not to say overworked, ingredients that had been so imaginatively treated in *Luke* — rebellion against authority, an existentialist posture and the ultimate triumph of defiance even in death.)

Paul Newman has always thrived on the interaction of working with other fine actors, and the cast of *Cool Hand Luke* was full of them. Though the star was nominated for the fourth time for an Academy Award, he again failed to receive one, the winner in 1967 being Rod Steiger for his work in *In The Heat Of The Night*. However, George Kennedy deservedly won an Oscar for his supporting performance, and there was a consolation for Paul — he won the Golden Globe Award as the World's Favourite Actor.

If, after having conquered yet again the peaks of critical

and commercial success, Paul might have been expected to fail in any attempt to surpass *Cool Hand Luke*, his choice of a farcical comedy — his fourth — for his next picture proved as disappointing in practice as it was predictable in terms of an actor's need for variety. For *The Secret War Of Harry Frigg*, released in 1968, was not even good of its kind — a tired, overly familiar tale of a military misfit not unlike Rocky Graziano whose larcenous talents are employed by the army, weary of his misdemeanours, to spring five one-star generals from imprisonment in Italy during World War II. Very eventually, Harry Frigg (Paul) engineers their escape, at the same time capturing for himself the love of an Italian *contessa* (a highly decorative Sylva Koscina). It is a long 110 minutes to the end of the picture, and if Jack Smight's direction had been sluggish in *Harper*, it is positively flaccid in *The Secret War Of Harry Frigg*. Even so, the script by Peter Stone and Frank Tarloff would have lacked lustre in the hands of any director.

The acting-honours are stolen by the ever-reliable Vito Scotti as an Italian colonel, but if Paul's performance is largely a recapitulation of the more obvious moods and mannerisms of Rocky Graziano, it is enjoyable in its own somewhat self-indulgent fashion.

Nevertheless, he was breaking no new ground, and he had complained, if with resignation, about the paucity of good scripts. It began to look as though it was time for Paul Newman, after twenty-seven films, to have a rest, take stock and think extremely carefully about picture number twenty-eight.

Few, though, could have guessed at the nature of his next project.

10

Regeneration And Rebirth

The careers of both Joanne Woodward and Paul Newman possessed built-in ironies that were not hard to spot. On the one hand, Paul, having begun in the cinema with a spectacular flop, had forged steadily ahead, his progress never seriously in doubt, to become the world's leading male-star, but he had given at least four superb performances — in *The Hustler*, *Hud*, *Hombre* and *Cool Hand Luke* — without being presented with an Academy Award. He could, of course, afford to laugh at the omission — even though the Oscar had the special distinction of being awarded by a star's hypothetical peers. In any case, others, apart from the self-hypnotic Academy Awards committee, showed their appreciation of his achievements: in 1966, as previously mentioned, he was named the World's Favourite Actor at the thirty-third annual Golden Globes banquet (Natalie Wood was the female counterpart); and in 1967, he was nominated Best Actor of the Year by the National Association of Theatre Owners. There were other honours, and he had garnered the sort of reviews that would keep him warm for the rest of his life.

Joanne, on the other hand, had won her Academy Award for *The Three Faces Of Eve* near the outset of her career and had afterwards gone largely unappreciated — certainly undervalued. Neither she nor Paul was anxious to admit the unpalatable truth that her professional life was not all they had hoped it would be. Suitable roles had been hard to find, and when they had presented themselves, they had frequently and disappointingly been in good pictures like *The Stripper* and *A Fine Madness* that were nonetheless poorly received. Furthermore, Joanne had in a way started at the top, so that there was an almost inevitable sense of anticlimax about much of what followed. For example, even though, as a whole, *The Three Faces Of Eve* had been sadly mismanaged, her role had provided a rare, perhaps unique opportunity, and she had more than met the challenge, making the film her own in a way that had simply not been possible in subsequent productions.

In 1967, it was announced that Joanne had been signed to an exclusive contract with Universal — a statement that was later retracted, though without any apology or explanation. The episode might have been interpreted as one more sign of problems in a career that gave the appearance of becoming confused and failing to realize a glorious potential.

Joanne had consistently refused to think of herself as a star, and she was searching hard for a good role — one in which she could immerse herself without unadventurously and safely repeating an earlier performance. In 1958, nearly a decade previously, she had forthrightly declared her own views of herself and her talent during a *Picturegoer* interview: 'I'm not a personality, like Audrey Hepburn or somebody. . . . If anybody's going to come and see me it's because they expect me to be a different character from the last one. And to the best of my ability I'm always going to be. Besides, because I'm not a personality, unless I'm a character, I'm nobody. This is why I went from the three different people in *The Three Faces Of Eve* to the Southern floozie in *No Down Payment* to the frustrated spinster in *The Long Hot Summer*. . . . In any cinema sense of the word, I don't believe I have a personality of my own. I take on the colouring of people around me. I wasn't in England a week before I was talking with a British accent. . . . People are always sending me scripts. The character is always either a Southern floozie or a neurotic. They don't understand — I've *been* those people, so I can't be them again.'

Full of self-knowledge, it was a brave artistic credo, and in the years that followed she had stuck to it without compromise, even though her insistence on virtuosity or the scope for it had made her screen-appearances comparatively infrequent and had propelled her into one or two doomed experiments such as *The Fugitive Kind*. But at least they had been experiments — not first carbons of previous successes.

Just when it looked as though her career might be entering an unmistakable slump, Joanne and Stewart Stern, who had some twelve years before written the screenplay of *The Rack* for Paul, discovered Margaret Laurence's *A Jest Of God*, a novel that they read while it was still in galleys. Joanne was immediately excited about the prospect of filming it, and Stern set to work on a screenplay. But the problem would be to find backers. Even coupled with the name of Joanne Woodward, the picture, as anybody could see, was going to be 'small' and subdued in its appeal — a doubtful commercial venture. Without really liking it, Paul had read the novel, but a number of factors were beginning to coalesce. He agreed to act as producer. For a long time, he had pondered the idea of directing a feature-movie, and the shift from producer to producer-director seemed a logical one, particularly as his wife and Stewart Stern were experiencing difficulty in finding backers. He decided to take the chance, and needless to say, *Rachel, Rachel* (as it was called in the end), even though Paul Newman as a director was virtually an unknown quantity, then assumed *some* attractions as a commercial property, so that Warners put up the money — just over $700,000. (Soon after the film's completion, it was estimated that it would gross better than seven million.) The picture could be made for the proverbial song because Paul and Joanne agreed to take no salaries, so fierce was their commitment, and because it was filmed to a tight schedule of five weeks.

Most people accepted that *Rachel, Rachel* was Paul Newman's first venture into directing. In fact, he had independently produced and directed a twenty-eight-minute short in the late fifties (the only Paul Newman film of any kind that the present author has not seen). On paper, this was a fairly austere exercise — Chekhov's monologue *On The Harmfulness Of Tobacco*, filmed in black and white and acted by Michael Strong, the fine player who has given excellent performances in such films as William Wyler's *Detective Story* and innumerable television-productions. Chekhov's piece involves the solo character in what is ostensibly a long lecture on the evils of tobacco but essentially, if contrapuntally, a protracted complaint about his wife. The filmed version was shown very briefly in art-houses but might accurately be described as a lost movie. For Paul, it helped feed an appetite that was already there.

'I've always wanted to direct,' he told journalist Jane

Wilson during the making of *Rachel, Rachel,* 'because I've always enjoyed most the peripheral things about acting, the rehearsals and the field-trips, the exploration of character, and the whole intellectual exercise of the thing.' Yet while dubbing himself 'cerebral' as an actor, he asserted that his direction was instinctive.

In most ways, the making of *Rachel, Rachel,* if by no means unique, was at least unusual. For example, Paul's editor, Dede Allen, one of the best cutters in the business, worked with him throughout, instead of being called in, as was customary, to edit the film after shooting had ceased. Filming took place in Danbury, Connecticut, and turned out to be largely a family-and-friends affair. Frank Corsaro, who had directed *Baby Want A Kiss,* was in the cast, Joanne of course played Rachel, Paul was behind the camera, and the infant Rachel was played by Joanne's firstborn, Elinor, using the pseudonym Nell Potts, a family nickname. One of the associate producers was Arthur Newman, and those seeing the two brothers together for the first time marvelled at their similarities and dissimilarities. Though not unlike him in appearance, Arthur had neither Paul's improbable degree of handsomeness nor his brother's seeming imperviousness to advancing years. One or two people found out, however, that his voice over the telephone was disconcertingly identical to Paul's.

A great believer in *non*-professionals as extras, Paul nevertheless chose for his own picture players of some experience whom he borrowed from the ranks of the local dramatic society. In so doing, he was not exactly hedging his bet but acting on a principle that he summed up thus: 'I've always noticed in my films that the less professional the extras are the better.' Shooting took place in the summer of 1967, but *Rachel, Rachel* was not released until almost a year later. Like that for the earlier *On The Harmfulness Of Tobacco,* the production-company was called 'Kayos'. Paul had wanted 'Chaos', but his manager, refusing pointblank to go along with the perhaps slightly sophomoric joke, had insisted on a less conventional orthography.

For Paul, the making of *Rachel, Rachel* was a great, revivifying experience. His professional life had assumed, for him, a *déjà-vu* aura that he categorized by saying that however positively the public reacted to his performances, he had reached a point at which he felt 'burned out creatively'. He was over forty, he had accomplished a great deal, and it was time for a break — a departure that would lend new impetus to his artistic drive. *Rachel, Rachel* provided that departure. Would it have done so if the film had turned out to be a failure or merely a so-so success? Probably yes. The change of direction was more important than worldly attainment.

The picture tells the story of Rachel Cameron, a primary-school teacher in a small New England town during what she calls her 'last ascending summer' before the watershed of thirty-five. With her demanding mother, she lives over a funeral-parlour and leads a predictable, restricted existence. This unspectacular pattern is disturbed when she has an affair with Nick Kazlik (James Olson playing a typical Newman part — the cynical, tender, deceiving loner), who had been a contemporary of Rachel in high school and who eventually lies to her that he is a married man and a father after perceiving that her feelings have deepened to a point at which he feels threatened. When he leaves town, his visit to his parents over, Rachel believes she is pregnant — only to find that her symptoms have been produced by a cyst that she has surgically removed. Made stronger by her experiences, she decides to break the monotonous rhythm of her life by moving to a new job in Oregon, taking her reluctant mother with her.

More than deft and sure, Paul's direction reveals great sensitivity and a true understanding of the characters involved as friendship, religion and love all fail Rachel in turn. This is a quiet, wistful picture with a quality that is almost pastoral, yet its gentle melancholy is lightened by a humour that the director never overplays. Paul shows that he is not afraid of stillness and silence. Without falsifying, Gayne Rescher's camerawork produces beautiful images, and the expected rapport between Joanne and her husband ensures that her performance, one of her best, steers the difficult course between self-pity and self-mockery. Her acting by-passes and transcends even the slightest caricature of spinsterhood. Thanks to the shrewd observation of the director, the town itself comes across almost as a character in the film — never either sentimentalized or dramatized. In retrospect, the love-affair may have its sordid overtones, but the picture depicts it for what it is — essentially a lyrical interlude in the heroine's life. *Rachel, Rachel* remains at all times a restrained, intimate, personal movie — one of which Joanne later said to Rona Jaffe, 'It was private, like life.'

Almost unanimously, the critics raved about the picture. Ten years after *The Three Faces Of Eve*, Joanne was again nominated for an Academy Award, as were the film itself, Stewart Stern and Estelle Parsons, who had memorably played Rachel's friend. The New York Critics' Awards for 1969 were to go to Joanne as best actress and to Paul as best director — just to make the honour greater, for the same picture. (For the Newmans, winning because of work on separate productions could scarcely have produced a comparable thrill.)

In the midst of all the excitement, one critic hung on to her cool. Pauline Kael, who had recently castigated Paul for criminally wasting himself in *Harry Frigg* at 'a time when he (was) physically right for a great role like Tommy Wilhelm in Saul Bellow's *Seize The Day*', was also one of the few reviewers to have reservations about *Rachel, Rachel*. Less than five years later, however, her praise for Paul Newman as the director of *The Effect Of Gamma Rays On Man-In-The-Moon Marigolds* was to be little short of extravagant.

But *Rachel, Rachel* was a triumph, and the Newman-Woodward partnership had scored a hit in a way that nobody had ever predicted. Beginning to receive many offers to direct, Paul hung on to *his* cool and waited for an attractive property. With his status and reputation, the pressure that might once have made him rush into a new venture was off; but a different kind of pressure, concomitant with spectacular success, was building up.

It was a busy time. Like the lives of so many other big stars before him, his existence was filled with wheeling and dealing — perhaps too much for his own taste. As an actor, he was about to make his first film for the Newman-Foreman Company, and in June, 1969, with Barbra Streisand and

Sidney Poitier (a trio that was joined by Steve McQueen in
1971), he would launch First Artists Production Company
Limited, a body that would handle the financing and distribution of productions in which the stars themselves would
appear. With Joanne often included in the business-structure,
these associations and alliances, plus others with Jennings
Lang, Stuart Rosenberg and George Roy Hill, demanded
time and energy at least in terms of discussions and setting
up the deals in the early stages. The results, however, included such films as *Winning* (a Jennings Lang Production produced by John Foreman), *Butch Cassidy And The Sundance
Kid* (a George Roy Hill-Paul Monash [Campanile] Production produced by John Foreman and directed by George Roy
Hill), *WUSA* (a Rosenberg-Newman-Foreman Production),
Sometimes A Great Notion (a Newman-Foreman Production;
a Jennings Lang Presentation), *Pocket Money* (First Artists/
Coleytown Productions) and *The Sting* and *Slap Shot* (both
of which were directed by George Roy Hill). Needless to add,
among these productions were two or three of the most commercially successful films Paul Newman would ever make,
but their head-spinning credentials make one aware that in
some ways so-called independent production was considerably less simple than the 'bad' old days of the big studios.

Whether life had become too busy for his taste or not,
Winning was to find Paul the actor at his most relaxed and
assured, and Joanne joined him, their confidence as a team
heightened by their recent success.

Winning had a long history that began in 1967 when it
was mooted as a television-movie to be presented by NBC-TV
as one of MCA's 'World Première' series. Part of the idea was
to make use of some hair-raising footage that was shot later,
in 1968, when the Memorial Day Indianapolis 500 had to be
aborted and started afresh after a seventeen-car pile-up. But
with Paul and Joanne heading the cast, *Winning* far outgrew
its relatively small beginnings and became by the time of its
release in 1969 a $7,000,000 feature for which Paul received a
colossal $1.1 million.

It was not an outstanding picture, and his participation
might have seemed enigmatic to those unaware of his growing passion for cars and speed that was to become even

stronger in the early seventies when he started to race seriously. As a hobby, he had already been driving fast for most of his adult life. At first, motorbikes catered to his craving until he gave them up in favour of cars after skidding on an oil-slick on Sunset Boulevard — an accident that caused injuries serious enough to keep him in hospital for a short while. As his stardom grew, he also became famous for driving a souped-up Volkswagen with a Porsche engine, and his addiction to speed increased, since he found in it release and relaxation — almost a form of therapy. *Winning* would give him a bag of money and the chance to have fun racing cars — circumstances that Steve McQueen, another motor-fanatic, would virtually duplicate for his 1972 film, *Le Mans*. Paul's picture would also give his co-producers the chance for heart-failure, for he refused to have a double for some sequences, and as a result, Universal had the star insured for $3 million.

In preparation for *Winning*, Paul went to the Bob Bondurant School of High Performance Driving in Santa Ana, California, as did also Robert Wagner, his co-star. Bondurant, who had been World Manufacturers' Champion in 1965, had previously coached Yves Montand and James Garner for John Frankenheimer's *Grand Prix*, and the master taught Paul to lap at 143 m.p.h. at Indianapolis, attaining a maximum of 160.

The racing is certainly the liveliest aspect of *Winning*, though otherwise the picture is not entirely without merit. Howard Rodman's screenplay is written to a classic formula almost as old as motion pictures themselves — boy meets girl, boy loses girl, boy gets girl back again. This ancient tale, however, is played out against a background of professional motor-racing, with the 500 as a climax to the drama. An ambitious driver, Frank Capua (Paul), meets a woman called Elora (Joanne) after a victory-celebration. They fall in love and soon marry, Frank establishing a healthy rapport with Charley (Richard Thomas), Elora's son by a previous union. But when Elora is almost inevitably neglected because of the demands of Frank's career, she begins a relationship with Luther Erding (Robert Wagner), Capua's friend and rival. Frank's response is to leave her, but when Charley is puzzled by his giving up so easily, Frank, having won the 500, returns to Elora for a fresh start. The fabric is thus extremely simple, but it is made somewhat diffuse by James Goldstone's lifeless direction, which seems more preoccupied with visual effects than the generation of excitement on or off the track. The film's strength, however, lies in the performances of Paul and Joanne, both of whom manage to convey far more than is in the writing. Paul's acting has maturity and quiet authority, and his looks, no longer quite so unnervingly time-defying, heighten his aura of experience and prove a better-than-ever register of such emotions as disillusionment, tenderness and resolution. Never finer than in his scenes with the boy, his acting is spare and without tricks. Joanne complements her husband in a manner that recalls *The Long Hot Summer*, the best of their earlier films made together.

Reviews seemed to indicate that Paul and Joanne were seen ever more distinctly by most commentators as Hollywood's 'golden couple' — not merely because of a marriage of durable contentment and an ability to stay out of sensational head-lines but also because they were attempting in their profes-sional lives to keep standards high, to do work that was unusually worthwhile. Even if *Winning* had hardly fallen into that category, Judith Crist, while spotting all the clichés, declared her willingness to stand and listen, enthralled, should the Newmans desire to do nothing more creative than read the telephone-book.

But there was a countercurrent, hostile to Paul and Joanne, maintained over many years by those jealous of the marriage whose battle-cry changed from 'It can't last!' only to 'It's all over!' or 'They're washed up!'. After *Rachel, Rachel*, the professional teaming of the Newmans was unassailable, at least temporarily. But the marriage, always fair game for a certain type of columnist, had been coming in for a con-centration of gossip and rumour — most of it unsympathetic.

Fact had nothing to do with the matter. For if we recall the words of Melville Shavelson quoted earlier, 'In Holly-wood rumours carry more weight than fact'; and in the scandal-sheets of Hollywood, New York and the rest of the world, more knives were flashing than in Alfred Hitchcock's *Psycho*.

At last, in July 1969, at a cost of more than $2,000, Paul

and Joanne took a half-page ad in the *Los Angeles Times*
spelling out the message: 'We are not breaking up.'

To outsiders — 'civilians', as they are sometimes called by
those in showbiz — what took place might seem incredible,
like a scriptwriter's wildest invention. But it happened.
('When you write straight reporting about the motion-picture
business,' Pauline Kael says in *The Citizen Kane Book*,
'you're writing satire.')

Because of the Newmans' dignified reticence, one can only
speculate about the feelings that had driven them to their
defensive action — the amused tolerance, perhaps, increas-
ingly tinged with irritation; then the anger, frustration and
hurt; finally the resolve to publicize a statement in order to
deny the calumny. For a while, the half-page ad subdued, if
it did not completely silence, the malicious chatter, but it
was gradually to build up again, the crescendo reaching its
height in the mid seventies, when there was once more talk
about single beds and public rows. This time, Paul and
Joanne endured the sniping of the gutter-press without resort-
ing to the sort of contradiction they had inserted in the *Los
Angeles Times.*

It is hardly surprising, then, that Paul has maintained over
two decades his defensive-aggressive attitude to newspaper-
men and that both he and Joanne cherish a privacy that can
be frustrating and even baffling for their most fervent
admirers.

On the whole, however, 1969 was a good year. As if in
defiance of the doom-merchants, Paul and Joanne embarked
on a second honeymoon during which they again visited
England.

One of their stops was at Stratford-upon-Avon, where they
attended the Royal Shakespeare Theatre and saw one of
England's most accomplished actresses, Judi Dench, as Viola
in *Twelfth Night*. Nearly ten years later, Miss Dench had
vivid memories of the Newmans' visit: 'I remember us all
being very excited by the fact that they were there, and
during the interval, I heard that they would both like to
come back and see me. I had a very, very small bit of false
nose just across the bridge of my nose, and a short wig over
my own hair. I rushed to my dressing-room as soon as the

curtain was down and took off the false bit of nose and put some make-up there so they wouldn't notice.

'They were extremely charming and sweet and said they had had a nice time. Paul Newman was relaxed, and we talked about the play as theatre-people.

'After they had gone, I didn't bother to comb my hair as I had to rush over to the Dirty Duck (a slightly esoteric term for a pub near the theatre called the Black Swan) to meet some people. I told them I was sorry to be late but Paul Newman and Joanne Woodward had been in to see me. My friends said yes, we know, and motioned to the next table, where they were sitting having a drink.'

Joe Cocks, the Stratford photographer, also has humorous recollections of that night. To take the pictures included in this book, he went backstage at the Shakespeare Theatre, where he is no stranger since he frequently photographs the productions and has many friends among the actors and staff. On that occasion, somebody waved him through a door with an encouraging, 'Go straight ahead, Mr Cocks,' and Joe, electrified, found himself on stage in the middle of *Twelfth Night*.

Always one to relish a good story, even one against himself, Joe caps that anecdote with a confession about Joanne: 'I thought she was very good-looking, but I thought she was just Mrs Newman. I didn't realize until later what a marvellous actress she was.'

The stage, particularly the Shakespeare productions on his own doorstep, preoccupies Joe almost to the exclusion of the cinema, but once more, Joanne's reiterated point is illustrated: it is hard, especially when one has a separate and glittering career of one's own, to live in the shadow of a superstar, to be 'just Mrs Newman'.

Having developed his pictures, Joe Cocks was pleased enough at least by one of them to think of getting Paul to autograph a print. Armed with the best of the bunch, he went next morning to the hotel in which the Newmans were staying near Stratford, knocked on their bedroom-door and, when Joanne answered, explained his mission. She disappeared for a moment with the photograph, but when she came back, Paul's signature was on it.

Joe Cocks had been spotted by the driver of the hire-car the Newmans were using during their stay in England, and when the photographer re-emerged from the hotel, the driver asked him where he had been. Exhibiting his trophy, Joe told him.

'Well, I'm damned,' said the driver. 'You're a lucky man. That's the first autograph he's given since he arrived in England.'

It may also have been the last.

In the States, as he had been in 1968, when he campaigned energetically for Senator Eugene McCarthy in the run-up to the presidential election and also served as a delegate to the national Democratic convention, Paul was active politically. In his home-state of Connecticut, he promoted Joseph Duffy in his candidacy for the US Senate. Strong political partici-pation, it was said, was a sure way for a star to make enemies, but Paul had never been afraid to do that. Perhaps he was no John Russell, the character he played in *Hombre*. There was, however, more than a little of John Russell in his sturdy independence. Such political activities were self-rewarding, but a special honour for the Newmans came in 1969 when they were presented with the William J. German Human Relations Award of the American Jewish Committee.

In October, Paul made one of his rare appearances on television when he acted as host and narrator for *From Here To The Seventies*, a two-and-a-half hour special NBC News Show in colour on the state of the nation. His involvement (Joanne once said, 'He fights for causes he thinks are valid. He cares') made him a logical choice for anchor-man.

Most obviously, that year was a good year professionally for Paul. As he was to be again in 1970, he was No. 1 at the US box-office, and much of the reason for his popularity was *Butch Cassidy And The Sundance Kid*.

For whatever combination of reasons, audiences loved the film, which took well over $30 million and eventually became the highest grossing Western in the history of motion pictures.

Can you quarrel with that sort of success? Well, there was much to pick holes in. For a comedy-spoof, *Butch Cassidy* was both insubstantial and inflated – a commercial bonanza made up of all-too-recognizable styles, some amiability and a near-total lack of unifying attitude to flimsy material. The laughs came thick and thin, while the moods had an easy familiarity, directed by no sustained emotion or thesis. True feeling, in fact, is what is so conspicuously absent from both *Butch Cassidy* and its companion-piece, *The Sting*. Director George Roy Hill builds both of them on charm or — even more insubstantially — on the *assumption* of charm, and Paul fits into them effortlessly, hitting his public again and again with that seductive smile that is ultimately meaningless, just something its owner forgot to turn off, and, worse, is duplicated on these occasions by Robert Redford's equally winning expanse of fine teeth. Even when we are entertained, seeing these movies is like eating large hunks of *Schwarzwaldertorte*: pleasant enough, but not really doing us any good. However, mindless times were on the cinema, and both *Butch Cassidy* and later *The Sting* were doomed to succeed.

One can hardly blame George Roy Hill for putting his energies into such properties. In *Period Of Adjustment* and *Toys In The Attic* (1963), he had shown perception and taste, but he has pointed out that his own two favourite pictures, *Slaughterhouse Five* and *The World Of Henry Orient*, fared worst at the box-office. Full of wit, invention and tenderness, *Henry Orient* was among the finest films ever made about children, but in movies excellence and success are too often different phenomena, and via the more commercial *Thoroughly Modern Millie*, the final cut of which was wrested away from him by the studio, Hill moved on to the smash-hit of *Butch Cassidy And The Sundance Kid*. When he, Redford and Newman decided to team up again for *The Sting*, it was with the idea of having fun in a minor work. For all its commercial prospects, the magnitude of the movie's ultimate earnings took the trio by surprise.

On the other hand, the popularity of *Butch Cassidy* was easier to analyse — at least after the event. Audiences were turned on by the Newman-Redford alliance, wittily defined by David Shipman as 'a sort of cool, straight Western version of the old Crosby-Hope relationship'. (While the picture was still a project and Paul was contemplating the casting of his partner, Steve McQueen, Warren Beatty and Marlon

Brando had all been considered.) For all its uncomfortable similarities with *Bonnie And Clyde*, William Goldman's face-tious script secured its laughs, even if their hip cues were as anachronistic as Paul's line: 'Boy, I got vision. The rest of the world wears bifocals.' The film was good to look at, and it had a hit-song, Bacharach and David's 'Raindrops Keep Falling On My Head', even if it was sung inconsequentially over an episode in which Paul comically rode a bicycle — a shameless borrowing from Truffaut's *Jules Et Jim*, which *Butch Cassidy* resembled in several other ways. As for the picture's sobering freeze-frame ending, it was worthy of better material.

(In an interview with *Screen International*, George Roy Hill explained its genesis: 'It was about halfway through the filming that I got the idea of stopping just before the bullets hit and leaving [Butch and Sundance] in almost mythic form. Originally, there was going to be a shoot-out to the end, but I have no stomach for real violence. My back was out when I was working on the film, and so they padded me around on a stretcher. While being driven to and from location, I man-aged to figure out the whole ending, and I don't think I would have done so had I not been so incapacitated.')

Despite mixed reviews, *Butch Cassidy And The Sundance Kid* enhanced the reputations of all concerned. After he had been penniless and unemployed, his career at crisis-point, the movie turned Robert Redford into a star or even a super-star. The British Film Academy voted him the year's Best Actor, with co-star Katherine Ross as Best Actress. Much of Redford's success was attributable to Paul Newman, both for selecting him and for generously bouncing dialogue off him in a way that enabled the younger actor to demon-strate his very considerable gifts.

But Paul had his reward, too. *Butch Cassidy* had made him No. 1.

A lesser man might have played things safe, might have succumbed to the understandable temptation to repeat him-self and look only for commercially sound properties. Indeed, there *were* signs that in recent years, Paul, having conquered his particular world, was relaxing. But in choosing *WUSA* for his next project, he ran a great risk with an unusual picture, lost the gamble and so went spectacularly down the chute from his biggest success to his greatest flop.

Costing nearly $5 million, *WUSA* died the death in both the US, where Paul took the—for him—unusual step of promoting it through personal appearances, and in Great Britain, whither Joanne travelled in 1971, the year following its release, in an attempt to stimulate business for the picture there. During her visit to London, Joanne said tactfully on one occasion that Paramount was 'not happy with it' and had thus been apathetic in promoting *WUSA*. In another, more forthright interview, she remarked, 'It is not a perfect film, but it does have something to say. I'm extremely offended by the way it was handled.' For his part, Paul considered that this, 'the most significant film (he had) ever made', had been the victim of political enemies, since its views were fundamentally liberal and anti-fascist.

Perhaps so. It might have been almost reassuring for Paul's admirers to think so. On the other hand, as those who saw this little shown picture soon realized, *WUSA* is woefully misconceived—turgid in its dialogue, inept in its narrative style and somewhat hysterical in its liberal attitudes. Crippled from the start by Robert Stone's script, Paul gives a good performance against the odds as a self-styled 'survivor', a cynical newscaster with a right-wing radio-station (call signal WUSA) in New Orleans, a man who has failed at marriage and as a musician. Joanne plays an ex-prostitute, a casualty who eventually hangs herself by a chain in her prison-cell, and Tony Perkins is a political fanatic. Extravagantly written though the roles are, both players do well but are swamped in the end by wild scenes that Stuart Rosenberg either cannot or will not control, culminating in a patriotic rally, an assassination attempt and a bloody riot. Even compared with the gaudy *The Left-Handed Gun*, this is probably Paul Newman's most reckless, overwrought and ostentatious film.

Nevertheless, his sincerity had been beyond question, and his disappointment at its failure was bitter.

Nor did he find his next picture, begun in mid 1970, so much more gratifying. *Sometimes A Great Notion* (also known as *Never Give An Inch*) ran into difficulties soon after shooting had started on 22nd June on location in Newport,

Oregon. Dissatisfied with the way in which the original director, Richard Colla (who went on to make the appallingly
turgid *Zigzag (False Witness)* in the same year), was handling
his subject, Paul fired him after three weeks of filming and
himself took over direction. But when he broke his ankle in a
motorcycling-accident, the inevitable delay pushed the production over budget, and the final cut was not ready until
late 1971, by which time Universal, through whom the
Newman-Foreman Company had arranged distribution, were
uncertain of how to market it, thus setting the seal on its
eventual financial failure.

In a sense, it was the *WUSA* story all over again, but *Sometimes A Great Notion* is a rather better picture. John Gay
finds in his screenplay a relatively simple cinematic equivalent for Ken Kesey's congested novel, and the plot is arresting and unusual, depicting the lives of the Stampers, a family
of lumberjacks who live with unyielding pride and independence. When a local strike takes place, their simple morality
brings them into conflict with the rest of the community,
whose hostility they defy, only to be seemingly defeated by
natural disaster. A snapping tree mangles the arm of Henry
Stamper (Henry Fonda), the father, and he dies as a result.
The same accident drowns one of his sons, Joe Ben (Richard
Jaeckel), and on the very day of the two deaths, Hank (Paul),
the older son, is deserted by his wife, Viv (Lee Remick). After
a bout with the bottle, Hank decides to fulfil the Stampers'
contract — to the incredulity of the townsfolk, who believe
that the struggle is ended. With the help of his half-brother,
Lee (Michael Sarrazin), he floats the full quota of logs down-
river, unbroken by the terrible events.

The general effect of the picture is slightly confusing, as if
key-scenes had been excised to leave motives unclear. Viv, for
example, potentially the most interesting character, never
fully emerges. Presumably, her dissatisfactions with the
Stampers are intended to be not merely a reaction to their
overt anti-feminism but also a moral commentary on their
whole way of life. But too little time is allocated to her growing frustration, and she is gone all too quickly, leaving the
audience puzzled by her choosing that particular day to
depart. Similarly, Lee — the feminist, hippie and odd man

out — finally throws in his lot with Hank for reasons that are not readily understandable. Furthermore, though he does a most creditable job, Paul's attitude as director to the material is not always clear, though those who condemn the film for its *political* content demonstrate nothing more than their own narrowmindedness and intolerance. (If anything, the picture is *pro*-integrity rather than *anti*-union.)

Paul directs with great visual flair, and all the performances are good — especially, given the circumstances, his own. He makes no attempt to soften the harsh virility of Hank Stamper, the insensitivity of the character that turns his strength into a vice, almost an extension of his physical arrogance. He is notably fine in the splendidly handled scene in which Joe Ben drowns — a sequence that begins in comedy as the trapped Joe Ben, cradling a huge log in his lap, relishes the ridiculousness of his predicament, and ends in tragedy as, despite Hank's valiant attempts to maintain mouth-to-mouth respiration, his brother perishes in the rising water. As the patriarch, Henry Fonda gives a typically sound performance of quiet authority, and Lee Remick invests Viv with a purity of sensibility that is largely unaided by the writing. There is a luminous quality to her acting that lingers in the memory.

Whatever flaws the film as released manifested, Paul's efforts as director were heroic. Lee Remick summed up thus her experience in working on *Sometimes A Great Notion*: 'Paul played an enormous role in the film, and also directed it, as there were serious difficulties with the original director. As an actress, I found his sensitivity as a director no surprise because of having worked with him as an actor, but the special understanding of actors' problems and his way of dealing with them was a great treat. It's a part of his professional life I would like to encounter again.' Once more, Paul had demonstrated that the talent shown in *Rachel, Rachel* was true and durable, its excellence to be observed in what was in some respects essentially a salvage operation, for he himself had explained that *Sometimes A Great Notion* was not the sort of material he would have chosen to direct.

Joanne, meanwhile, had followed *WUSA* by pursuing the separate strand of her solo career in another Newman-Foreman production, *They Might Be Giants*, a fantasy which at least one critic found utterly beguiling and perceptive, despite a distributor's cut that threatened its coherence. Joanne's performance and that of George C. Scott were highly praised, but Joanne herself was to describe the film as 'an absolute horror'. Virtually driven into retirement by the experience, she was not to re-emerge for two years — and then to be directed by her husband. Of *They Might Be Giants*, she said, 'It was the most miserable experience I've ever had, making that film. I hated it. It would be pointless to go into the reasons now, although I must say that they had nothing to do with George Scott, who was a perfect gentleman throughout. But there was a time when I said I would never make another picture as long as I lived, and I really didn't want to work for a long time.'

There had been no consolation at the box-office, either, and yet a third Newman-Foreman production released in approximately the same period ran into trouble. This was *Puzzle Of A Downfall Child*, starring Faye Dunaway, Viveca Lindfors, Barry Morse and Roy Scheider — an unusual project but a resounding flop. But, for Joanne, since the experience was so highly personal, the traumatic one of the three was *They Might Be Giants*.

11

Where Next?

Joanne's trip to England in the autumn of 1971 confirmed her status as the more approachable of the two Newmans. She had always given excellent interviews, and if she was not actually the darling of the British Press, they certainly devoted a generous amount of column-inches to her. That November, her short visit had the purpose of promoting the ill-fated *WUSA*, but journalists proved less interested in the picture than in Joanne Woodward herself, who obligingly produced her invariably articulate remarks not only about *WUSA* but also about Paul Newman, thirteen years of marriage and her own character just across the threshold into the forties.

What was she like, then, at forty-one — the mother of three, the wife of the world's most popular and successful moviestar, the actress who had a formidable career in her own right?

Speaking of her marriage, she quoted the words of her friend Peter Ustinov, who had once said that she and Paul had managed to 'shut out the draughts of difference'. It was certainly true: the Newmans thrived on having interests that might have seemed to outsiders to be diametrically opposed; they basked in the warmth of possessing complementary characters, much more positive and negative than the carbon-copy personalities that could sometimes be seen in other happy marriages. Occasionally, a modicum of missionary zeal might be at work — not always successfully. For example, describing herself as a 'balletomaniac', Joanne had been working hard at ballet since her late thirties and had tried repeatedly to get Paul to attend classes, arguing that for so physical a person it was a good way of working out. Paul refused. It wasn't simply that he hated ballet; he also had an accurate awareness of the fact that he would look ridiculous in tights. Some men — Errol Flynn, for instance — had faces and figures that were timeless, belonging to no particular century, and thus Flynn in doublet and hose, far from provoking laughter, had had women sighing over his masculine beauty. There could be no doubt that Paul had stimulated his share of sighs, but his face and figure slotted into a time-span that extended only from the late nineteenth century up to the present, and he was not about to be seen, even if only by fellow-dancers, looking laughable in tights with legs that he described as skinny.

Similarly, Joanne had failed to convert him to the joys of needlepoint, even though it was, she asserted, conducive to relaxation and despite the fact that Henry Fonda, indubitably masculine, went in for it. While she was busy with her classes, Paul would shoot pool or play tennis, but although he preferred to attend fights or car-races, he would go to ballet-performances just to be with her. Conversely, Joanne, loathing skiing, would go on skiing holidays with him just so that they could spend their nights together. For the previous two years, she had been practising piano and guitar — musical interests that were not shared by Paul, either.

Her grandmother, from whom Joanne had inherited many traits of character, had told her that the test and gauge of marriage was the simple ability to enjoy talking across the breakfast-table for fifty years to the same man. It was an old-fashioned view, of course, but Joanne, reared in a respectful southern tradition, had never forgotten the words. She cherished Paul's different inclinations and took nourishment from them, as he did from hers. That attitude had kept their marriage going — plus the fact, she would add in dry tones, that she loved him and adored him.

As for the Newmans' life-style, it was unspectacular: they lived relatively quietly, with a small group of friends among whom they would exchange visits. Such domesticity had its negative aspects, the worst being, as Joanne saw it, a public image the virtue of which was little short of dour. With a well-developed sense of humour, she thought that the impression of sweetness and light, if not misleading, was far too sober and overlooked their humanity, their fallibility and their instinct for fun. For that reason, she had liked the picture of the two of them that had adorned the cover of *Life*. It had made her look, she said, like Agnes Moorehead, not a bit like the little woman who doted uncritically on her sex-symbol husband.

Of her family, she spoke unashamedly with a mother's pride. Nell (Elinor) was by that time twelve and still a film-star, having recently been in a television documentary, *The Eagle And The Hawk*, about endangered species of birds. She was a falconer, and while she was in London, Joanne would buy for her a volume on falconry. Lissy (Melissa) was nine, and her talents included cooking, painting and writing music. As for Clea (Claire), she was a precocious five-year old who had scarcely shaken off an addiction for the trampoline. Although Joanne's heart would always be with her family, she would later talk in less than rosy terms about parenthood, the drift of her argument being that for an independent woman it could prove too constricting. As if unconsciously to demonstrate that her own vision took in far more than conventional domesticity, she told one journalist that besides the book on falconry for Nell, she had bought new volumes on Nijinsky and Rudolf Nureyev. (She has her own print of the Nureyev-Fonteyn film of *Romeo and Juliet*.)

Ironically, though Joanne was about to terminate her short visit and fly home for Thanksgiving, giving thanks, with memories of *WUSA* and *They Might Be Giants* fresh in her mind, formed no great part in her talk about moviemaking. Sounding frankly disenchanted, at least for the moment, she explained, 'Making movies is not fun any more. You get no sense of joy. Too many practical considerations. No one enjoys it now. It is like grim death if the sun goes down early and they lose half a day's shooting. They get ulcers and worry about going $2,000,000 over the budget. . . . Acting should be a matter of fun and games, but even in films, it's not as much fun as it used to be. There's no such thing as a picture that does okay any more: it's either an enormous hit or an absolute bomb. So nobody will let you take a chance, and you've got too much riding on you. It's exhausting.'

One interesting loose end was left in her conversation. She mentioned that her next film would probably be Peter Ustinov's adaptation of Iris Murdoch's *A Fairly Honourable Defeat*, but the picture was never made.

If success is one of the two great obsessions of the twentieth century, nobody, in worldly terms, stays at the top for ever, and by 1971, Paul Newman had already slipped to No. 3 at the box-office.

First Artists, founded in 1969, had yet to produce a picture. Explaining the company's aims, Paul had said, 'The motion picture industry can and must be streamlined. For too long, we have lived with outdated production and distribution. The purpose of this company, among other things, will not necessarily be to economize, but to put production on a more efficient basis. The money belongs on the screen.' These had been brave words, possibly prompted to some extent by Paul's anger that the low-budget *Rachel, Rachel* had nonetheless incurred high administrative and distribution costs.

By 1971, he had yet to put his plans to the test, and the various projects planned for that year never saw the light of day. These included *Where The Dark Streets Go*, in which Paul would star as a priest, and *Hillman*, the story of a man living in a house he had constructed from garbage. In the event, First Artists' premier production was equally unusual and surprising. Originally announced as *Jim Kane*, it was finally released in 1972 as *Pocket Money*, a gentle, wry and understated comedy, in which Paul was teamed with Lee Marvin. Completely failing to come to terms with this quietly original picture, *Variety* suggested that it was an abortive attempt to repeat the success of *Butch Cassidy And The Sundance Kid*, but the two films had very little in common. Undeservedly, *Pocket Money*, directed, like *WUSA*, by Stuart Rosenberg, was Paul's third commercial failure in a row, virtually confirming Joanne's hypothesis about enormous hits and absolute bombs. In a healthy cinema, there should have been room for a small, unemphatic film of this kind.

The contemporary story, brilliantly scripted by Terry Malick from J. P. S. Brown's novel, was photographed in masterly fashion by Laszlo Kovacs in Tucson, Arizona. Paul and Lee Marvin played two amiable losers who have gone to Mexico to buy cattle. With more than a touch of larceny, Marvin, an inept hustler, persuades Paul that the Mexicans can be swindled, but predictably it is the two slow-witted, incompetent Americans who turn out to be the dupes and lose all their money. Typical of the film's ironic humour is Marvin's remark as he surveys his proposed victims: 'I advise you not to spit around here. You might hit a sucker.' The partnership of Newman and Marvin works superbly. Paul gives another relaxed, unshowy performance, not afraid to allow Lee Marvin to register strongly in a role that is all bluster and hot air. These are characters who live in a fantasy and are incorrigible, despite the fact that the world is continually yanking out the rug from underneath them. As well as the fine acting of the principals, *Pocket Money* contains an admirable character-sketch from Strother Martin, who had also given sterling service in *Cool Hand Luke* and *Butch Cassidy*. Of all Newman pictures, *Pocket Money* is the one most likely to be overlooked in any discussion of the star's work. It deserved a better fate.

For *The Life And Times Of Judge Roy Bean*, released in the same year as the previous film, Paul returned to Arizona, where shooting took place in the desert near Tucson. This 'romp' or 'lark', as director John Huston called it, perhaps in self-exculpation, was to do poorly at the box-office — the second First Artists production to fall short of expectations. It was an uneasy mixture of fact and legend, comedy and brutality, romance and deflating anti-romanticism. Even technically, as the mike-boom repeatedly dropped into shot, the film proved a surprising disappointment.

There was, of course, a Roy Bean, one of the larger-than-life figures who flourished ubiquitously in the West of the late nineteenth century. He was born in Kentucky around 1825 and later drifted about California and Mexico. From the early 1880s until he died in 1902 (a date somewhat alarmingly changed to 1925 in John Milius' screenplay for *The Life And Times*), he was 'the Law West of the Pecos' in Langtry, a dot on the map of West Texas that he had renamed for the great passion of his life, Lily Langtry. Bean had previously been played by Walter Brennan, who won an Academy Award for his performance in William Wyler's *The Westerner* (1939), and by Victor Jory in Budd Boetticher's *A Time For Dying* (1969).

Milius appears to get his ideas from other movies as much as from the facts or legend, and even the opening title: 'Maybe this isn't the way it was—but it's the way it should have been' is reminiscent of *Butch Cassidy*'s preamble: 'Most of what follows is true'. Riding into Vinegaroon, which he is later to rechristen after the Jersey Lily, Roy Bean is immediately set upon, beaten and hanged—saved from death only by the breaking of the rope. He returns, shooting all and sundry in revenge, and sets himself up as 'Judge', the town prospering under his rule until at last the community turns against him and he rides away disillusioned. After twenty years, he comes back to rid Langtry of gangsters, and he dies gloriously beneath a blazing oil-derrick.

Huston can do little with his material, which is as full of mayhem as it is devoid of characters. Not even Roy Bean has coherence, and he is hard to admire, not merely dispensing justice in quirky fashion but also alienating the audience as much by his buffoonery as by his brutality. The episodic nature of the story has no convincing logic, and vignettes by Stacy Keach, Ava Gardner and Huston himself only emphasize the gaudy nature of the proceedings—all manner and very little art.

Though he is upstaged by a bear called Bruno, Paul makes a valiant effort as Roy Bean. He has a full beard and a gruff, rather expressionless voice. Essentially, the part is a character-role, and here lies the probable explanation of Paul's interest. Once more, even if in an unfortunate context, he demonstrates his versatility. Though the part ultimately defeats him as it is written, Roy Bean is about as far away as he has ever been from either Newman the screen-idol or Newman the man. He had explained ten years earlier his attraction to playing such roles as Juan Carrasco or the Battler: 'The character of the young lawyer that I played in *The Young Philadelphians* was much closer to me as a human being—and much duller—than Eddie Felson, the character I played in *The Hustler*, in 1961. But the characters that are farthest away from my own personality are the ones I feel most successful with.'

Nevertheless, whatever his feelings about his own performance as Roy Bean, which was praised by some critics who thought the film as a whole extremely weak, Paul could not have been happy about the reception of *The Life And Times Of Judge Roy Bean*. As if to underline the point, somebody dreamed up the story of fundamental disagreements between the star and John Huston. Paul was quick to deny that he would rather have directed the movie himself, saying that he had long desired to appear in a Huston picture. Just to settle the matter beyond any doubt, his next role was in Huston's *The Mackintosh Man*. Ironically, however, it was yet another failure, a glum affair that could not transcend an inferior screenplay.

As a footnote to *The Life And Times Of Judge Roy Bean*, it might be added that Pauline Kael found the picture all the more disheartening because Paul, who was becoming well known for his interest in ecology and problems of energy and the environment, had involved himself in what he was intelligent enough to see was a right-wing fantasy that revelled in wholesale destruction.

However, Miss Kael found herself able to respond a good deal more positively to his next venture.

After *Rachel, Rachel*, Paul had considered producing in England a film based on *Precious Bane* in which Joanne would have starred, but nothing came of the idea. However, finding promising material in Paul Zindel's Pulitzer Prize-winning play, *The Effect Of Gamma Rays On Man-In-The-Moon Marigolds*, he decided to direct Joanne once again in a film-version, with John Foreman producing. Scarcely recognizable chewing gum and in curlers, Joanne played Beatrice Hunsdorfer, a veritable monster among mothers.

Beatrice, a middle-aged widow who had been deserted by her husband before his death, lives in a run-down house with her two daughters, Ruth (played by Roberta Wallach, daughter of Eli Wallach and Anne Jackson), a selfish, boy-crazy teenager who is also an epileptic, and Matilda (Nell Potts), the younger daughter, intelligent and introverted. (It is her experiments on mutation in marigolds that give the piece its ungainly title.) Beatrice is a self-disgusted slut who treats both girls badly, but it is clear that Matilda will do better than survive, even though the drama ends after she has returned from winning first prize at her school's science fair only to discover that Beatrice has killed her pet-rabbit.

Without either fully disguising its theatrical origins or converting the second-rate into the first-rate, Alvin Sargent opens out the play in his adaptation and reduces its claustrophobia. Though neither writing nor direction attempts to deny that Beatrice is impossible and insufferable, the film allows its audience to glimpse the forces that have made her what she is, and if she never even approaches sentimentality, Joanne's acting reveals the vulnerability that is also in the character. The two daughters are well contrasted: Ruth, though she incurs her mother's wrath by imitating her to schoolfriends, is clearly doomed to become a first carbon of Beatrice; Matilda, on the other hand, surpasses all that is best in her mother and has a mature wisdom that almost reverses their roles in the family. Since Matilda is played by a picture-stealing Nell Potts, who in real life is the daughter of her screen-mother, Joanne Woodward, it is hardly surprising that Nell manifests many of the qualities that have revealed themselves in Joanne's more sympathetic characterizations. Looking at Matilda/Nell and seeing resemblances to Beatrice/Joanne, despite or because of their dissimilarities in the film, one is irresistibly reminded of the lines:

Thou art thy mother's glasse and she in thee
Calls back the lovely Aprill of her prime.

There is not a bad performance in *Moon Marigolds*, but possibly because of the bravura nature of Joanne's role, it is the quiet understatement of Nell's playing that proves most effective — a skill she has clearly inherited from her mother and father.

Paul's direction does wonders with a play that has too many echoes of other — and often better — plays. It would be hard to deny that the characters and situations have a tired familiarity. Since his début, Pauline Kael pointed out, he had obviously learned an immense amount about making movies. 'He's an unobtrusive director,' she went on, 'keeping the camera on what you'd look for in the theatre;

his work is serene, sane and balanced.' Furthermore, the picture gains enormously from the way in which obvious big scenes are avoided or toned down. It is a film of peripheral excellence, in which the best sequences turn out to be interpolations to the original play. One of these is a fine scene in which Beatrice encounters a policeman at dawn and they recognize each other as old schoolmates – sad, funny, embarrassing.

Artistically, *Moon Marigolds* must have satisfied all the Newmans, perhaps especially the thirteen-year-old member of the trio. But although reviews were sympathetic, the picture did not do well.

In other ways, at least for Joanne, it had proved expensive. Beatrice Hunsdorfer was not a character whom she could leave on the set, where, incidentally, she and Paul had some dandy fights. 'I was so depressed and suicidal during that film I couldn't stand it,' Joanne said. 'I hated the way I looked. I hated that character – what she did to her children. At home, I was a monster, and Paul and I avoided each other as much as possible.'

As she thought and felt herself into the personality of this woman who had alienated her children, did her 'sense-memory', one wonders, go back to the times after her marriage when there were problems with the children – especially Scott and Susan – of Paul's first union?

For the best part of ten years, if *Winning* was overlooked, she had not been allowed to appear glamorous on the screen, and after the dowdy Rachel and the slatternly Beatrice Hunsdorfer, a more prepossessing character would have been a welcome change. For her next role, she had her eye on the part of Ann Stanley, the beautiful forty-year-old divorcée in *40 Carats*. After all, if Ingrid Bergman could score a hit in exactly the same type of characterization in *Cactus Flower*, Joanne could certainly play Ann Stanley. However, the role went to Liv Ullmann, Joanne commenting wryly, 'No one could see me as a forty-year-old sexpot except Paul.'

Refreshing though the change might have been, the lead in *40 carats* was not, artistically, the biggest deal in the world. At least *Summer Wishes, Winter Dreams*, Joanne's next picture, was to secure for her the New York Critics'

Award and an Academy Award nomination. It was probably just as well. Playing Rita Walden in menopausal crisis had not been, on the face of it, much of an escape from depressing parts in which Joanne had depicted 'women in frayed bathrobes'.

Originally to have been entitled *Death Of A Snow Queen*, Gilbert Cates's *Summer Wishes, Winter Dreams* was a maudlin soap-opera in which the 'snow queen' Rita, though stylish and personable, paraded her neuroses with hardly a trace of the humour that is usually to be found somewhere in any Joanne Woodward performance. Stewart Stern, who adapted *Rachel, Rachel*, wrote *Summer Wishes, Winter Dreams* and crammed it with problems that might have come out of an updated Joan Crawford movie. Rita's long-standing frigidity towards her husband, her discovery that her son is a homosexual, the death of her mother after a heart-attack that failed to convince Rita, her squabbles with her daughter about the rearing of her grandson — these are some of the items in a catalogue of factitious and improbable woes. *Summer Wishes, Winter Dreams* was a sad picture, all right; but not in the way that its makers had intended. Despite a respected award, the role seemed a waste of Joanne's talents.

Meanwhile, Paul's career was still on a downhill slide that was not arrested by John Huston's *The Mackintosh Man*, released in 1973, the same year as Joanne's latest picture. Underscored by the director's undisguised enthusiasm for his star, the reunion of Newman and Huston could have been seen as full of promise. When critic David Robinson visited the unit at Pinewood Studios, England, he witnessed the shooting of a scene in which Paul waited to be rescued under a prison-wall. After the take, Huston walked over and addressed a few words to his star, before retiring to watch the next take. To Robinson, he remarked, 'Just now — this is when you're really in touch with an actor — I saw the way that was done, and I said, "Paul, try to be invisible when you come over." That's all. That's all you have to tell him. He is really extraordinary.'

Such praise seemed auspicious, but *The Mackintosh Man* was to disappoint expectations, not least commercial ones.

Though filmed with some narrative skill and a feeling for locations, the story is dull, the characters no more interesting than the situations in which they find themselves, and the plot-twists of a kind to provoke sighs. All these shortcomings might not have mattered so much if the hero played by Paul had been more three-dimensional and had appeared in a more sympathetic light. But insofar as his character emerges at all, he is a weary, cynical professional who exhibits no concern for the ethics of his profession until the final moments of the picture. Spy-movies could be thrilling, like *North By Northwest*, witty, like *Our Man Flint*, or philosophical, like *The Spy Who Came In From The Cold.** Being none of these, *The Mackintosh Man* has little to commend it — not even a fine performance from Paul, a fact that, given the script, was hardly difficult to understand. His acting was subdued and without animation, as grey as the skies over Ireland, where much of the film was shot, presumably because of Huston's fondness for his homeland. To set the seal on a near-disaster, the score by Maurice Jarre was appalling. This was Paul's sixth flop in a row, and his popularity had declined correspondingly.

Never content to be just a moviestar, Paul found consolation in a variety of activities, notably motor-racing. Pushing fifty, the very age at which most drivers considered retiring, he had begun to race in earnest. In April 1971, he had narrated for ABC-TV *Once Upon A Wheel*, a special about the automobile-sport in which he appeared with various champions of the track and with Glenn Ford, James Garner and Kirk Douglas, who took part in a Pro-Am event at Ontario Motor Speedway in California. But being little more than an active fan could not satisfy Paul for long. *Winning* had provided some sort of outlet for his enthusiasm, but the experience had been too directly geared to stardom. In the early seventies, he took up the sport seriously, and by 1974, he was good enough to win two national championship races driving a Datsun. In the same make of car, he would at

---

* Made, interestingly enough, by Paul Newman and Martin Ritt. 'We sold the company,' Ritt said later, 'to raise some money.'

least once, even though he emerged unscathed, come very close to death.

Why the fascination for high-speed driving? 'I love racing', he once stated simply. 'I wish I could devote every minute of my time to it. To be behind the wheel of a car doing well over 100 mph is one of the most exhilarating things I know of.' (By contrast, both he and Joanne, mindful of conservation, drive small cars on the public highway.)

The hobby he had begun to pursue so seriously, however, though it accurately indicated the dispersion of his interests, was by no means a sign that he was in semi-retirement. He had begun to relax, yes; and relaxation had something to do with his next great success. But if anybody thought that Paul Newman was washed up or had given up, he had *The Sting* to reckon with.

12

The Jackpot and the Marriage-Stakes

Almost everybody has heard of *The Sting*, and most people, it would sometimes appear, have seen it. If made for fun, it was also made for money — a slick, commercial entertainment that did huge business. Useless, then, to point out that the story is preposterous and the plot full of holes, that Robert Redford is too old to be a naïve kid and that Paul is somewhat young to be playing an old con-man emerging from retirement to engineer one last big score. It is almost as though there is an unconscious parallel between the role he plays and Newman at forty-seven: his performance is effortless and assured in a part that requires no effort; he looks young and handsome enough to pull off any swindle requiring charm and good looks — impossibly, age-defyingly, heartbreakingly young and handsome; and he shows every sign of happiness and good spirits. It is likewise futile to point out that Scott Joplin died in 1913, that his rags had been popular well before the mid thirties in which the action is set and that their use in the film, reworked by Marvin Hamlisch, is both anachronistic and a blatant attempt (it worked) to cash in on their revived vogue in the seventies. But tinkering with age and time comes as readily to the picture as seductively suspending disbelief on the part of its public. Aside from being nudgingly full of wipes and irises, outmoded devices to remind us that *The Sting* is set in 1936, the film is nonetheless impersonally directed by George Roy Hill, who has made no apparent attempt to curb the arch *camaraderie* of the two principals — the slightest of variations on their roles in *Butch Cassidy And The Sundance Kid*. Visually, however, there is a small but striking change to epitomize the cuteness of the production: Paul now has the moustache that Redford wore in the earlier film. *The Sting* wends its course over more than two hours and is an amazingly bland concoction — just right for the amoral seventies, into which it also fits neatly by being devoid of women in any significant or essential sense. It was probably enjoyed by exactly the same public who had enjoyed *Butch Cassidy*, and just as *The Sting* was hard to take seriously, so it was hard to castigate sternly those who lapped it up in such large numbers. In any case, to do so was like running down Santa Claus.

The picture served to revive Paul's depressed fortunes, though there were those who, predictably, asserted that Redford, not Newman, was the great box-office draw.

By the time *The Sting* was released in 1973, however, what was perhaps more interestingly observable was the way in which Redford was coming if not to live in the shadow of Paul Newman, then, whether by choice or not, to conform to a pattern that the older star had firmly established. Between *Butch Cassidy* and *The Sting*, Redford had made seven films, out of which *Tell Them Willy Boy Is Here*, *The Downhill Racer* and *Little Fauss And Big Halsey* were all failures, while his popularity enjoyed a resurgence through *The Hot Rock*, *Jeremiah Johnson*, *The Way We Were* and *The Great Gatsby*. At the same time, he had established himself, no matter how sharply defined his screen-persona, as an elusive personality, as private as Paul Newman, with whom he shared, among the comparatively small amount that was known about the two men, the following other traits: he was an ecologist and conservationist; as a lover of seclusion, he was a stern custodian of his family's anonymity; he was hypersensitive about being valued for his good looks; and he was conspicuously faithful in his marriage. If Robert Redford had consciously set out to model himself on Paul Newman, he could hardly have done better.

From one big commercial hit, Paul went straight to another, maintaining and enhancing his popularity even though the picture in which he appeared had little merit beyond the dubious attractions of sensationalism. When Fox and Warner discovered that they were contemplating projects that were virtually identical, they joined forces to make *The Towering Inferno*, its very title suggestive of amalgamation, since it derived directly from two novels upon which Stirling Silliphant's screenplay was based — *The Tower* and *The Glass Inferno*. The film came in the midst of the cycle of disaster-movies that spawned, among others, *Earthquake* and *Jaws* and provided entertainment for audiences made up of jaded people of the crudest sensibility. Delighted by their profits, moviemakers overlooked the fact that their success was based on a system of diminishing returns, that they could not endlessly cap with new horrors the sick delights of allowing the public to witness the full detail of people being burned to death, devoured by sharks or crushed by falling buildings. Furthermore, it could be argued with some force that a cinema exploiting the perverse and morbid appeal of disasters was in no sense healthy, especially since it was attracting a mass-audience by no means habitually hooked on movies that would soon drift back to its television-receivers and, sad to relate, similar real-life events brought to them in the comfort of their own homes.

In essence, *The Towering Inferno* is inflated hokum that tells, over 165 minutes, how the Glass Tower, the world's tallest building at 138 storeys, burns down in San Francisco. Any conceivable human interest comes a poor second to the technical effects. If Paul looks as handsome as ever in the picture, he also seems understandably ill at ease. He plays a designer and architect (conventional movie-shorthand for virile dreamer and man of vision) who has incredibly failed to notice the dangerous cutting of corners on a vast project. The last scene of the picture is a collector's item. After — through his own negligence and/or corruption — the tower-block has been destroyed and many lives lost, builder William Holden, presumably about to go to jail for an unspecified number of years, grins at Paul and says words to the effect: 'Let's build one bigger and better.'

In two ways, *The Towering Inferno* represented a watershed for the motion-picture industry. The huge public that paid money to see it as well as such films as *Airport* and *The Exorcist* were not turned on in the same way by *Earthquake*, *The Omen* or the sequels to *Airport*. Both *The Towering Inferno* and *Airport*, moreover, provided sad evidence that moviemakers were dancing on graves, for having selected stars like Paul, Steve McQueen, Faye Dunaway and Robert Wagner presumably for their drawing-power, they deliberately reduced them in status until they became mere bit-players, on the screen only for a limited period. *Airport* and *The Towering Inferno*, however, were arguably less significant than the later *Jaws* or the remake of *King Kong*, both of them devoid of stars or even the opportunity for good acting. If this was indeed a trend, the future for most stars looked even bleaker than it had become.

A lesser but interesting aspect of *Inferno* was the acting of one Scott Newman as a nervous fireman. The part was so small that it was hard to assess potential, but Scott had obviously inherited his father's good looks.

In the month after he finished filming, Paul had a characteristically busy time. He went to New York to introduce Ramsey Clark, the ex-Attorney General, at a fund-raising rally. With Joanne, he made a television-documentary on ecology. He managed also to fit in some motor-racing, a speech at a conference and some active work leading to a campaign to stop offshore oil-drilling in California. As if all that were not enough, he had begun rehearsals for his next picture and reached 175 mph in a Ferrari during a practice-run as a member of a team who were out to break the world speed-record.

Released in 1975, his new picture was *The Drowning Pool*, a sequel, after nearly ten years, to *Harper*. It did not, however, recapture the success of its predecessor, being a rather pointless exercise that was weak on atmosphere and directed in subdued fashion by Stuart Rosenberg. To movie-buffs, though, this First Artists production was of additional interest because so many reunions were to be observed. Besides joining with Rosenberg again as director and, as so often before, having his brother Arthur Newman as production-manager, Paul had selected among his co-players Richard Jaeckel, whose fine acting in *Sometimes A Great Notion* had secured an Academy Award nomination, and Tony Franciosa, the gifted actor with whom he had last appeared in *The Long Hot Summer* in 1958. Joanne was reunited with Paul in the picture, too, portraying his ex-mistress who commits suicide during the course of a bizarre series of events that fail to add up to a convincing or gripping mystery. Her role was neither large nor commensurate with her talent — though the second shortcoming was also present in

Paul's leading part. At least, though, Joanne looked beautiful, having remarked a year before, 'Perhaps I've played too many ugly roles in depressing films to acquire a famous face. But I never had Liz Taylor's kind of moviestar-looks.' Possibly not. But it could have been said that she had a much subtler beauty that added incalculably to the effectiveness of her playing, and in *The Drowning Pool*, she contrived once again to suggest a dimension in her role that was simply not present in the writing.

The year 1975 was marred by another ugly chapter in the Newmans' at best uneasy relationship with the Press, which at times took on the appearance of a running battle. Like a mongrel pack attempting to halt the progress of a royal couple by snapping at their heels, the newspapers were at it again, it seemed, in full cry after the Newmans, sustained in their pursuit by scraps of gossip. There was much talk, for example, of an uninhibited altercation between husband and wife in Sardi's New York restaurant. The report could have been accurate, but Paul and Joanne had never claimed that their shared life was one of uninterrupted serenity. On the contrary, their marriage was healthier because they aired their differences instead of bottling them up. The previous year, Joanne had told an interviewer that she and Paul had given up sleeping in a double-bed. Malicious commentators made what they could out of that confession, but Joanne had never said that the Newmans no longer shared a bed — merely that sleeping could be easier without one's partner. (The gossips conveniently overlooked her repeated deflating joke about Paul Newman sex-symbol: 'He's in his fifties, and he snores.') Many happily married couples decide after a time that double-beds no longer seem quite so inevitably attractive, and Paul and Joanne had been married for seventeen years. Nevertheless, the talk persisted, and as late as 1977, Joanne was still finding it necessary to say, 'I know there have been rumours, but there's no question of marital separation. I still love Paul, and he loves me. There's no split or anything like that.'

In 1975, Paul was probably far more concerned about his career than with any problems in his life with Joanne. Without finding what he was looking for, he was reading more scripts than ever and had expressed his intention of confining his energies more closely to direction. He even went so far as to say that he was bored with the characters he had been playing—a comment that would not raise eyebrows, however, after *The Mackintosh Man*, *The Towering Inferno* and *The Drowning Pool*.

In the spring of that year, he had been announced as cast for *A Bridge Too Far*, the blockbusting, soporific war-film in which his friend Robert Redford, not Newman, eventually appeared, receiving $2 million for twenty days' work. ('If people are foolish enough to offer money like that,' said Redford, 'I'd be a bigger fool to turn it down.') By the autumn, Paul was reported to have agreed to star in a movie-version of E. L. Doctorow's bestseller, *Ragtime*, with the pop-star Mick Jagger playing his son; but so far nothing has come of the project. Again, only a short time later, it was stated that Paul would for the third time in his acting-career essay a role with marked homosexual traits—on this occasion, as a track-coach in love with a long-distance runner training for the Olympics. (In the plot-details, there are superficial resemblances to a situation depicted in Michael Winner's 1969 film, *The Games*.) He has as yet not played the part, though reports say that the project is still under consideration. It will be remembered that homosexuality had been part of the make-up of the characters Paul portrayed in the film *Cat On A Hot Tin Roof* and the play *Baby Want A Kiss*.

Instead of any of these roles, Paul chose to play William F. Cody in the self-indulgent film directed by Robert Altman and self-indulgently titled *Buffalo Bill And The Indians, Or Sitting Bull's History Lesson*. Even though he was acting one of the character-parts he so relished, it is hard to see what Paul hoped would come out of this venture. He might, however, have failed to allow for Altman's wayward talent and a final screenplay in which the director himself had a hand. Faintly ominously, a credit informs the audience that the script is 'suggested by' the original play.

In October, 1969, the Newman-Foreman Company had paid $500,000 for the drama *Indians* by Arthur Kopit. On stage, Stacy Keach had played William F. Cody, the role that Paul would re-create on the screen. With the lapse of time, however, it had seemed as though the whole project had fallen through. It might, indeed, have been better if it had, for *Buffalo Bill*, a static, over-emphasized and repetitive work, debunks a hero and a myth for two long hours. Paul's appearance recalls a stage-direction in Edmond Rostand's *Cyrano De Bergerac*, in which one of the principal characters enters 'magnificently grown old'. Altman had compared Cody in his film to Willy Loman in Arthur Miller's *Death Of A Salesman* — an accurate parallel in terms of rhetoric and sententiousness. But despite the gaudy script, Paul is good. While Cody is all that is base, Sitting Bull is all that is noble. Paul, however, comes close to redressing the imbalance of this simple-minded proposition, for his Buffalo Bill is moving in his corruptness and pathetic fallibility. Emblematically, he is of course the superior white race that has committed genocide on the Indians, and thus, ten years later, Paul has moved over from John Russell's position in *Hombre* to represent all the evil humbug of those who condoned and applauded the slaughter of the Sioux.

By this time, Paul needed a hit again, but he did not rush the search, and his next screen-appearance found him taking life easy, without dialogue, in Mel Brooks's *Silent Movie*. As unequal as most of Brooks's pictures, this one was enlivened by guest-cameos featuring Paul, James Caan, Burt Reynolds, Liza Minnelli and Anne Bancroft (Mrs Mel Brooks). In his own episode, Paul was seen being chased through the grounds of a hospital by Brooks, Marty Feldman and Dom DeLuise, all of them driving motorized wheelchairs — a funny, if slightly heavy-handed, satirizing of Paul's preoccupation with motor-racing.

Agreeable though this sort of thing might be, it was clearly nothing more than a marking-time in the Newman career. Paul was hungry to act again in a worthwhile picture, and he might have thought he had the chance with *Slap Shot*, released in 1977, breaking away from the persona to which his public would willingly have confined him. For one who resented being regarded as a personality-star, it was an enormous relief, and yet in the later years of his career, he admitted that he had been more discriminating in his choice of directorial assignments than in picking his acting-roles.

The title of the film refers to a somewhat wild shot in ice-hockey that usually fails to find the goal. Though he still looks young, even with grizzled hair, Paul plays Reggie Dunlop, the ageing player-coach of the Charlestown Chiefs, a bottom-of-the-league ice-hockey team in Pennsylvania that appears to be facing disbandment. When the general manager Joe McGrath (the excellent Strother Martin yet again) signs up the Hanson brothers, a bizarre-looking trio, Reggie is puzzled—until he sees them play with dirty tactics that are outrageous even by the standards of a violent and cynical sport. As a result, though, the Chiefs win their match and, playing dirty, begin to recoup their fortunes.

This outline makes *Slap Shot* sound like yet another seventies *macho*-movie in which anything goes in a rotten world— much the same sort of thinking that had been apparent in George Roy Hill's *Butch Cassidy* and *The Sting*. But *Slap Shot* is significantly different. The film sets up its heroes if not the more successfully to knock them down, then the more keenly to expose the often pathetic reality behind the *macho* façade. These revelations might be taken for a form of sentimentality were it not that Hill's direction, aided immeasurably by the tight editing of Dede Allen (Arthur Penn's preferred cutter, who had also edited *Rachel, Rachel*), moves the picture swiftly over any dangerous ground. No matter how good he is on skates, Reggie loves a wife (Jennifer Warren) whom he cannot keep because she refuses to be an 'ice-hockey widow', and he bolsters up his confidence with casual sexual encounters. The incongruously well educated Ned Braden (Michael Ontkean), the Chiefs' star, is unable to hang on to his wife, either, because he turns out to be frigid. Even the Chiefs' glory is hollow as well as corrupt: their anonymous owner, a tough businesswoman, is unmoved by their return to form and plans to write them off as a tax-loss.

Despite these seemingly sordid features and its length of over two hours, *Slap Shot* is fast, exciting and broadly comic. The speed is essential, for the ice over which the film skates, unlike that of its hockey-games, is often dangerously thin. Stylistically, the picture is far from assured, for all its professionalism, and its mayhem fails as slapstick, despite the brisk tempo, and more than tries tolerance if one takes it seriously. Furthermore, though both physically and in his acting Paul is excellent and well matched by a good cast containing several little-known players, the characters depicted do not exist convincingly as people. That Paul should have been attracted by the acting-opportunities presented by *Slap Shot* was understandable; but he was mistaken if he saw in the screenplay a fully worked-out idea with a consistent point of view.

The film's violence and — perhaps more especially — its uninhibited language alienated some critics and quite a few moviegoers. Paul defended *Slap Shot* vigorously, arguing that the violence was there, all right, but that it did not lead to killing or maiming, one of the sickening preoccupations of contemporary cinema, and that the bad language at least bore the stamp of authenticity. To *Photoplay*'s Vernon Scott, he said, 'Some people find the language in the picture a little rough. And it *is* rough. But I have a theory that if something is honestly, truly funny, then it isn't vulgar. It goes beyond those bounds. There's that kind of truth in *Slap Shot*.' He also admitted that the broadness of its humour reflected his own outrageous sense of the comic.

Since the picture could have been seen as inviting its audience to relish all the mayhem on ice even as they disapproved of it, some of his disclaimers might have sounded a little disingenuous. But whatever the weaknesses of *Slap Shot*, it showed, if there were any around who still doubted the fact, that Paul Newman could still give a fine performance in an unusual, unglamorous role.

He has been generous in his acknowledgement of debts. The Actors' Studio has helped him. Certain directors have assisted him enormously. But to a large extent, he has to be seen as somebody self-taught — the view that Harold Schonberg, writing of Bach, Mozart and Haydn, took of musical geniuses. 'They have minds like blotters', he said, 'that immediately soak up and assimilate. . . . They merely have to be pointed in the right direction and be given a little push.'

For a long time, Paul resisted life's little pushes. But in the end he got to where he was going rapidly enough.

13

A Big Hand for the Old Pro

In 1977, Paul Newman was a slightly improbable fifty-two —
in the finest tradition of those imperishable leading men
headed by such stars as Cary Grant and David Niven. Paul
celebrated his birthday at a party given by Joanne's old
friend Gore Vidal at a Hollywood house the writer had
rented.

At fifty-two, Paul *has* relaxed somewhat, as well he might.
The movie-business is fuelled by insecurity, but he has paid
his dues, as he would put it, and is old enough to do what
the hell he wants. As anyone interested knows, part of what
he wants is to enjoy the thrill of racing fast cars. In May
of his fifty-second year, undeterred by that particular feature
of the calendar, he took part in the taxing twelve-hour endurance race at Sebring, Florida, driving a Porsche 911S.
He has sometimes raced a Triumph TR–6 and was national
champion in Class D (small sports cars) production-racing.
In 1974, he won two national championship races driving
a Datsun, and last season he finished third overall in Class
B sedan-racing, in which he drove a Datsun 510. In 1975,
he also formed his own racing-team, P.L.N. He asserts that
the sport has been 'a lot of laughs', but it has given him
at least one big scare, too.

In the summer of 1977, he was again driving a Datsun
510, this time at a Sports Car Club of America race at
Garrettsville, Ohio, when another competitor's car flipped
into the air and landed on top of the Datsun. By some
miracle, neither driver was hurt. It was, however, a close
call for Paul, who was saved by his crash-helmet when the
roof of the Datsun collapsed under the impact. His safety-
harness also did its work well, if at the expense of bruising
around his neck and shoulders. Reportedly, once the dust
had settled and he had climbed out of his car, he swore
roundly at the other driver, Robert Dyson of Poughkeepsie,
New York, whose attempt to thrust through a gap in the

field had led to the accident when the race was a mere ten seconds and fifty yards old. But Paul's fit of cursing was no doubt an emotional reflex, because as soon as it was over, he went to check on Dyson's safety.

If that event was memorable for the wrong reason, Paul likes to look back on the Daytona 24-hour Endurance Race of April, 1977, in which, driving Clint Eastwood's Ferrari, he finished fifth.

As for Joanne, she would probably be much happier if her husband gave up racing altogether. When his temper flared after another track-incident at Lime Park, Connecticut, it was said that Joanne found a reason to leave the stands immediately — upset almost as much by her partner's public profanity as by his flirtations with danger. (Forced off the track by a rival, Paul made a gesture as eloquent as it was bawdy.) There has certainly been scant evidence that she enjoys watching the racing in which Paul now finds the stimulus that has almost inevitably faded somewhat from his activities as a star. However, if he combines, creatively and harmlessly, both racing and acting in First Artists' projected film *Stand On It*, a story of stock-car drivers, Joanne is likely to breathe a sigh of relief.

Though he hates being made to sound solemn, his political commitments are as strong as ever. He denies, however, being anti-establishment, arguing strongly that he is simply anti-corruption, anti-stupidity and anti-injustice. He is fond of calling himself 'an absolute square'.

With Joanne, Paul is working to help the Indians on the Bellingham Reservation. Yet another concern dear to his heart is the Washington Energy Action Committee, whose striving is directed towards the establishment of an informed energy-policy. It might be suggested that this is one way in which he fights on behalf of a younger generation — his own children and other people's.

In the spring of 1977, the Newmans flew into London so that Joanne could co-star with Laurence Olivier in a television-production of *Come Back, Little Sheba* by William Inge, the very dramatist who had, in a sense, through *Picnic*, brought her and Paul together. Though Paul would stay with her while the production was being filmed, they announced that Joanne would remain in England for a year while Paul gave his career a rest and looked after their three teenage-daughters in America. With a small glow of self-praise, Paul commented, 'It's a beautiful thing to do'; but he had also said, 'There aren't any new parts that excite me at the moment, so I'm in semi-retirement.' He left it to Joanne to stress that they were not separating in any dramatic or sensational sense and that her husband hoped, freed from motion-picture commitments, to involve himself more deeply in her wide range of interests.

For example, Joanne had recently been attending classes at Sarah Lawrence University, perhaps making up for those two years at Louisiana State when she had 'majored in parties'. She is active on behalf of Planned Parenthood, and she serves on the board of directors of the Manhattan Ballet Company. But despite all these causes and enthusiasms, she needed the time and release from domestic ties that would allow her to flex her personality a little more, to confirm her own separate identity. Not long before, she had again voiced her old complaint: 'The only time I'm recognized in public is when I'm with Paul. Even then, people aren't looking at me. They're looking at him.'

Paul understood. They would see each other from time to time, but he sympathized with her need for a break and a change, which complemented his own readiness to take a rest from hard, steady work, most of it on location. He would again get to know his children, who were rapidly growing up. As for his marriage, such a union of two gifted artists and strong personalities, each with a right to his own career and identity, inevitably had its stresses. But it had endured for almost twenty years, and both partners, despite Joanne's so-called 'year of grace', want it to continue. There is no chance, they insist, that Joanne's twelve months of freedom will have such a heady flavour that she will not wish to give up her liberty at the end of the period.

Joanne has been announced as co-star with Burt Reynolds in *The End*, which Reynolds will himself direct, but her latest appearance before a mass-audience at the time of writing was on January 8th, 1978, when 'Laurence Olivier Presents' screened *Come Back, Little Sheba*, directed by Silvio

Narizzano, on England's ATV network. With Olivier himself as her co-star in this, possibly William Inge's bleakest drama, Joanne played the sluttish and aimless Lola Delaney, who instead of aiding her reformed-drunk husband Doc (Olivier), is caught up in her own middle-aged romantic dreams. With her insubstantial yearnings and her lyrical, idealized memories of the past, she cushions herself against the truth that Doc was forced into marriage with her and that his disappointment at having to give up his medical studies helped to make him an alcoholic.

In this kind of role — as an eroded, physically unalluring woman — Joanne has always had her critics, notably Pauline Kael, who has declared herself resolutely unfooled by the actress's masking of her beauty. If the point is valid, it is also superficial. For ugliness, Joanne may indeed have to rely heavily on the make-up kit; but she has always excelled at depicting battered optimism and what has been called 'the sad business of making the best of a bad job'. Rachel Cameron and Beatrice Hunsdorfer in *Moon Marigolds* were roles that indicated how effortlessly Joanne would fit Lola Delaney into her remarkable range. In the event, her success in *Come Back, Little Sheba* was an even greater triumph because the character she played was considerably older than Rachel, Beatrice or Joanne herself.

Repeatedly calling for her missing dog Little Sheba (sym- bolically, the past), lagging behind her husband's stoical awareness that evoked Clough's lines —

But play no tricks upon thy soul, O man,
Let fact be fact and life the thing it can.

—Joanne as Lola was at once ridiculous and touching in her empty-headed longing for ancient glories, as vulnerable as she had earlier been in the film *The Stripper*. (Even the names of Inge's two characters, Lola and Lila, have a striking similarity, for they are sisters beneath the skin.) The oboe-quality of Joanne's voice conveyed more of hurt innocence than of frustrated childishness, and though her appearance might have seemed younger than the character's years, her negligent stance and slack way of holding her body created a telling illusion of physical degeneration and slatternliness. In a performance armed with the courage to be graceless, she memorably created Lola's eagerness to give and receive love, her only half-comprehending devotion to Doc.

In neither talent nor technique was there any sense of disparity between Joanne's playing and that of Olivier, and this television-production revealed her gifts at an apogee. That she should perform so well in a play by William Inge, in whose *Picnic* her career might be said to have begun, was fitting inasmuch as it closed the circle and summed up a quarter-century of distinguished work.

And what, today, of Paul Newman — the actor and the man?

He is sometimes hard to take seriously — an observation that he would probably accept as a compliment. He might, he suggests, become a marine biologist. As for his unfading good looks he boasts that he has a recipe. Every day, he puts on a snorkel and plunges his head into a pail of very cold water, keeping it there for twenty minutes. 'It tightens my skin,' he claims, 'better than any cosmetic, and it takes years off my appearance.'

Perhaps more in earnest, he mentions plans of directing Joanne in a film for television, a medium that he predicts will become more adventurous than films. Of what he himself will do as an actor in the future, he says little.

Some years before, he had remarked, 'I envy Laurence Olivier, because he seems to have endless resources in him to develop and be a different character each time. I feel I perhaps don't have the imagination to change.' Since one is *par excellence* a screen-actor and the other's sphere, despite great film-performances, has always been pre-eminently the stage, it is difficult to compare the two stars. But in the twelve years or so since he modestly made that statement, Paul has more than proved his own versatility and the creative resources he can bring to new, unusual roles. He has often told interviewers, 'I don't want to die and have written on my tombstone: "He was a helluva actor until one day his eyes turned brown".' Those eyes are still a heart-stopping blue, but sex-symbol or not, his epitaph could never, after

Hud, Hombre and *Cool Hand Luke*, be the one he once feared.

He continues to guard his privacy with all the old assiduity. His public does not really know Paul Newman the man, and probably they do not want to. They are happy enough with Paul Newman superstar.

After his hesitant, uncertain start in the fifties, Paul has been — primarily as an actor but also as a director — a key-figure of the sixties and seventies — scarcely the best era in movie-history or even one offering a diversity of roles or the secure system in which a star might at least establish himself as a personality-performer. Among both old and new stars, the casualty-rate has been spectacular. Yet Paul has done much more than merely imprint his personality on to the screen; he has proved himself, with sure emotional and artistic instincts, to be a notable interpreter. His durability is not in doubt. Although it comes perhaps as a shock to realize that he is well into his fifties, a star is nothing if not an eternal possibility. Paul Newman has surprised moviegoers before. Inferior though the films themselves were, his appearance as a character-actor in *The Life And Times Of Judge Roy Bean* and *Buffalo Bill And The Indians* suggests something of his future — a future which, for a star of such proven gifts, might well make the world gasp a little more.

Bibliography

Frischauer, Willi, *Behind The Scenes Of Otto Preminger* (London, Michael Joseph, 1973).

Hamblett, Charles, *Paul Newman* (Chicago, Henry Regnery Co., 1975; London, W. H. Allen and Co. Ltd., 1975).

Jaffe, Rona, 'A Weekend With Paul Newman'. *Good Housekeeping* October, 1969.

Kael, Pauline, *I Lost It At The Movies* (New York, Bantam Books, 1966; London, Jonathan Cape, 1966).

Kael, Pauline, *Kiss Kiss Bang Bang* (Boston, Little, Brown, 1968; London, Calder and Boyars Ltd., 1970).

Kael, Pauline, *Going Steady* (London, Temple Smith, 1970).

Kael, Pauline, *Deeper Into Movies* (Boston, Little, Brown, 1974).

Kael, Pauline, *Reeling* (Boston, Little, Brown, 1976; London, Marion Boyars, 1977).

Kerbel, Michael, *Paul Newman: A Pyramid Illustrated History Of The Movies* (New York, Pyramid Books, 1973; London, W. H. Allen and Co. Ltd., 1975).

Logan, Joshua, *Josh: My Up And Down, In And Out Life* (London, W. H. Allen, 1977).

Quirk, Lawrence J, *The Films Of Paul Newman* (New York, Citadel Press, 1971).

Robinson, David, 'The Innocent Bystander', *Sight And Sound*, Winter, 1972/3.

Ross, Lillian and Ross, Helen, *The Player: A Profile Of An Art* (New York, Simon and Schuster, 1962).

Sheppard, Dick, *Elizabeth: The Life And Career Of Elizabeth Taylor* (London, W. H. Allen and Co. Ltd., 1975).

Shipman, David, *The Great Movie Stars: The International Years* (London, Angus and Robertson Limited, 1972).

Thompson, Kenneth, *The Films Of Paul Newman* (Bembridge, Isle of Wight, BCW Publishing Limited, 1977).

Thomson, David, *A Biographical Dictionary Of The Cinema* (London, Secker and Warburg, 1975).

Tressider, Jack, *Heart-Throbs* (London, Marshall Cavendish, 1974).

Truffaut, François, *Hitchcock* (New York, Simon and Schuster, 1971).

Williams, Tennessee, *Memoirs* (London, W. H. Allen and Co. Ltd., 1976).

Wilson, Jane, 'Hollywood's Blue-Eyed Boy'. *Sunday Times* Colour Supplement, 7th January, 1968.

Filmography

(Where no colour process is indicated it may be taken that the film was made in black and white.)

PAUL NEWMAN AS ACTOR

[The titles of Paul Newman's films have frequently been changed, mainly for release in Great Britain. Where such changes have taken place, the revised title is indicated in brackets. Abbreviations: d—director; sc—script; l p—leading players.]

1. *The Silver Chalice*, Warner Brothers, 1954, Warnercolor; d Victor Saville; sc Lesser Samuels from Thomas B. Costain's novel; l p Pier Angeli, Virginia Mayo, Joseph Wiseman, Jack Palance, Alexander Scourby.

2. *The Rack*, MGM, 1956; d Arnold Laven; sc Stewart Stern from a teleplay by Rod Serling; l p Walter Pidgeon, Anne Francis, Wendell Corey, Edmond O'Brien, Lee Marvin.

3. *Somebody Up There Likes Me*, MGM, 1956; d Robert Wise; sc Ernest Lehman from the book by Rocky Graziano with Rowland Barber; l p Pier Angeli, Everett Sloane, Eileen Heckart, Harold J. Stone, Sal Mineo.

4. *The Helen Morgan Story (Both Ends Of The Candle)*, Warner Brothers, 1957; d Michael Curtiz; sc Oscar Saul, Dean Riesner, Stephen Longstreet and Nelson Gidding; l p Ann Blyth, Richard Carlson, Alan King.

5. *Until They Sail*, MGM, 1957; d Robert Wise; sc Robert Anderson from a story by James A. Michener; l p Jean Simmons, Joan Fontaine, Piper Laurie, Charles Drake, Sandra Dee.

6. *The Long Hot Summer*, 20th Century Fox, 1958, Eastman Colour; d Martin Ritt; sc Irving Ravetch, Harriet Frank Jr from material by William Faulkner; l p Joanne Woodward, Anthony Franciosa, Lee Remick, Angela Lansbury, Orson Welles, Richard Anderson.

7. *The Left-Handed Gun*, Warner Brothers, 1958; d Arthur Penn; sc Leslie Stevens from a play by Gore Vidal; l p John Dehner, Lita Milan, Hurd Hatfield.

8. *Cat On A Hot Tin Roof*, MGM, 1958, Metrocolor; d Richard Brooks; sc Richard Brooks, James Poe, from the play by Tennessee Williams; l p Elizabeth Taylor, Burl Ives, Jack Carson, Judith Anderson.

9. *Rally 'Round The Flag, Boys*, 20th Century Fox, 1958, Eastman Colour; d Leo McCarey; sc Claude Binyon and Leo McCarey from the novel by Max Shulman; l p Joanne Woodward, Joan Collins, Jack Carson, Tuesday Weld.

10. *The Young Philadelphians* (*The City Jungle*), Warner Brothers, 1959; d Vincent Sherman; sc James Gunn from Richard Powell's novel *The Philadelphian*; l p Alexis Smith, Barbara Rush, Robert Vaughn, Brian Keith.

11. *From The Terrace*, 20th Century Fox, 1960, DeLuxe Colour; d Mark Robson; sc Ernest Lehman from the novel by John O'Hara; l p Joanne Woodward, Ina Balin, Leon Ames, Myrna Loy.

12. *Exodus*, United Artists, 1960, Technicolor; d Otto Preminger; sc Dalton Trumbo from the novel by Leon Uris; l p Eva Marie Saint, Sal Mineo, Lee J. Cobb, Peter Lawford, John Derek.

13. *The Hustler*, 20th Century Fox, 1961; d Robert Rossen; sc Robert Rossen, Sidney Carroll from the novel by Walter Tevis; l p Piper Laurie, George C. Scott, Jackie Gleason, Myron McCormick, Murray Hamilton.

14. *Paris Blues*, United Artists, 1961; d Martin Ritt; sc Jack Sher, Irene Kamp, Walter Bernstein, from a novel by Harold Flender; adaptation by Lulla Adler; l p Joanne Woodward, Sidney Poitier, Diahann Carroll.

15. *Sweet Bird Of Youth*, MGM, 1961, Metrocolor; d Richard Brooks; sc Richard Brooks from the play by Tennessee Williams; l p Geraldine Page, Ed Begley, Rip Torn, Shirley Knight, Mildred Dunnock, Madeleine Sherwood.

16. *Adventures Of A Young Man (Hemingway's Adventures Of A Young Man)*, 20th Century Fox, 1962, DeLuxe Colour; d Martin Ritt; sc A. E. Hotchner from the Nick Adams stories by Ernest Hemingway; l p Richard Beymer, Diane Baker, Arthur Kennedy, Fred Clark, Jessica Tandy.

17. *Hud*, Paramount, 1962; d Martin Ritt; sc Irving Ravetch, Harriet Frank Jr from the novel *Horseman, Pass By* by Larry McMurtry; l p Melvyn Douglas, Patricia Neal, Brandon de Wilde, Whit Bissell.

18. *A New Kind Of Love*, Paramount, 1963, Technicolor; d Melville Shavelson; sc Melville Shavelson; l p Joanne Woodward, Thelma Ritter, Eva Gabor, George Tobias.

19. *The Prize*, MGM, 1963, Metrocolor; d Mark Robson; sc Ernest Lehman from the novel by Irving Wallace; l p Edward G. Robinson, Elke Sommer, Diana Baker, Kevin McCarthy.

20. *What A Way To Go!* 20th Century Fox, 1963, DeLuxe Colour; d J. Lee Thompson; sc Betty Comden, Adolph Green from a story by Gwen Davis; l p Shirley MacLaine, Robert Mitchum, Dean Martin, Gene Kelly, Dick Van Dyke.

21. *The Outrage*, MGM, 1964; d Martin Ritt; sc Michael Kanin from the play by Fay and Michael Kanin based on Akira Kurosawa's film *Rashomon*; l p Laurence Harvey, Claire Bloom, Edward G. Robinson.

22. *Lady L*, MGM, 1965, Eastman Colour; d Peter Ustinov; sc Peter Ustinov from the novel by Romain Gary; l p Sophia Loren, David Niven, Claude Dauphin.

23. *Harper (The Moving Target)*, Warner Brothers, 1966, Technicolor; d Jack Smight; sc William Goldman from the novel *The Moving Target* by Ross MacDonald; l p Julie Harris, Lauren Bacall, Arthur Hill, Janet Leigh, Robert Wagner, Pamela Tiffin, Shelley Winters.

24. *Torn Curtain*, Universal, 1966, Technicolor; d Alfred Hitchcock; sc Brian Moore; l p Julie Andrews, Lila Kedrova, David Opatoshu.

25. *Hombre*, 20th Century Fox, 1966, DeLuxe Colour; d Martin Ritt; sc Irving Ravetch, Harriet Frank Jr from the novel by Elmore Leonard; l p Diane Cilento, Fredric March, Barbara Rush, Richard Boone, Martin Balsam, Cameron Mitchell.

26. *Cool Hand Luke*, Warner Brothers, 1967, Technicolor; d Stuart Rosenberg; sc Donn Pearce, Frank R. Pierson from the former's novel; l p George Kennedy, Jo Van Fleet, J. D. Cannon.

27. *The Secret War Of Harry Frigg*, Universal, 1967, Technicolor; d Jack Smight; sc Peter Stone, Frank Tarloff from story by Tarloff; l p Sylva Koscina, Andrew Duggan, Vito Scotti, John Williams, Tom Bosley.

28. *Winning*, Universal, 1969, Technicolor; d James Goldstone; sc Howard Rodman; l p Joanne Woodward, Robert Wagner, Richard Thomas, Clu Gulager, David Sheiner.

29. *Butch Cassidy And The Sundance Kid*, 20th Century Fox, 1969, DeLuxe Colour; d George Roy Hill; sc William Goldman; l p Robert Redford, Katherine Ross, Strother Martin, Jeff Corey, Henry Jones.

30. *WUSA*, Paramount, 1970, Technicolor; d Stuart Rosenberg; sc Robert Stone from his novel 'A Hall of Mirrors'; l p Joanne Woodward, Tony Perkins, Laurence Harvey.

31. *Sometimes A Great Notion* (*Never Give An Inch*), Universal, 1971, Technicolor; d Paul Newman; sc John Gay from the novel by Ken Kesey; l p Lee Remick, Henry Fonda, Michael Sarrazin, Richard Jaeckel.

32. *Pocket Money*, National General, 1972, Technicolor; d Stuart Rosenberg; sc Terry Malick from the novel *Jim Kane* by J. P. S. Brown; l p Lee Marvin, Strother Martin, Wayne Rogers.

33. *The Life And Times Of Judge Roy Bean*, National General, 1972, Technicolor; d John Huston; sc John Milius; l p Jacqueline Bisset, Ava Gardner, Tab Hunter, John Huston, Anthony Zerbe.

34. *The Mackintosh Man*, Warner Brothers, 1973, Technicolor; d John Huston; sc Walter Hill from the novel *The Freedom Trap* by Desmond Bagley; l p Dominique Sanda, James Mason, Ian Bannen, Harry Andrews.

35. *The Sting*, Universal, 1973, Technicolor; d George Roy Hill; sc David S. Ward; l p Robert Redford, Robert Shaw, Charles Durning.

36. *The Towering Inferno*, 20th Century Fox/Warner, 1974, De-Luxe Colour; d John Guillermin; sc Sterling Silliphant from the novels *The Tower* by Richard Martin Stern and *The Glass Inferno* by Thomas M. Scortia and Frank M. Robinson; l p Steve McQueen, William Holden, Faye Dunaway, Robert Wagner.

37. *The Drowning Pool*, Warner Brothers, 1975, Technicolor; d Stuart Rosenberg; sc Tracey Keenan Wynn, Lorenzo Semple Jr and Walter Hill from the novel by Ross MacDonald; l p Joanne Woodward, Tony Franciosa, Richard Jaeckel.

38. *Buffalo Bill And The Indians, Or Sitting Bull's History Lesson*, EMI, 1976, DeLuxe-General Colour; d Robert Altman; sc Alan Rudolph and Robert Altman from the play *Indians* by Arthur Kopit; l p Joel Gray, Burt Lancaster, Kevin McCarthy.

39. *Silent Movie*, 20th Century Fox, 1976, DeLuxe Colour; d Mel Brooks; sc Mel Brooks, Ron Clark, Rudy De Luca, Barry Levinson from a story by Ron Clark; l p Mel Brooks, Marty Feldman, Dom DeLuise.

40. *Slap Shot*, Universal, 1977, Technicolor; d George Roy Hill; sc Nancy Dowd; l p Michael Ontkean, Jennifer Warren, Strother Martin.

41. *Paradise* (project), 1978.

42. *Stand On It* (project), 1978.

PAUL NEWMAN AS DIRECTOR

1. *On The Harmfulness Of Tobacco*, Kayos Productions, 1961; sc from the play by Anton Chekhov; l p Michael Strong.

2. *Rachel, Rachel*, Warner Brothers, 1968, Eastman Colour, print by Technicolor; sc Stewart Stern from the novel 'A Jest of God' by Margaret Laurence; l p Joanne Woodward, James Olson, Estelle Parsons, Nell Potts.

3. *Sometimes A Great Notion* (*Never Give An Inch*), Universal, 1971. (For details, *see* previous filmography.)

4. *The Effect Of Gamma Rays On Man-In-The-Moon Marigolds*, 20th Century Fox, 1972, DeLuxe Colour; sc Alvin Sargent based on the play by Paul Zindel; l p Joanne Woodward, Nell Potts, Roberta Wallach.

THE FILMS OF JOANNE WOODWARD

1955   *Count Three And Pray*
1956   *A Kiss Before Dying*
1957   *The Three Faces Of Eve*
       No Down Payment
1958   *The Long Hot Summer*
       Rally 'Round The Flag, Boys
1959   *The Sound And The Fury*
       The Fugitive Kind
1960   *From The Terrace*
1961   *Paris Blues*
1963   *The Stripper (Woman Of Summer)*
       A New Kind Of Love
1964   *Signpost To Murder*
1966   *A Fine Madness*
       A Big Hand For The Little Lady
1968   *Rachel, Rachel*
1969   *Winning*
1970   *WUSA*
1971   *They Might Be Giants*
1972   *The   Effect   Of   Gamma   Rays   On   Man-In-The-Moon
       Marigolds*
1973   *Summer Wishes, Winter Dreams*
1975   *The Drowning Pool*
1978   *The End* (project)

Index